Abstracts of the Deaths and Marriages in the
Hightstown Gazette

New Jersey

18 April 1861-28 December 1871

Richard S. Hutchinson

HERITAGE BOOKS
2007

HERITAGE BOOKS
AN IMPRINT OF HERITAGE BOOKS, INC.

Books, CDs, and more—Worldwide

For our listing of thousands of titles see our website
at
www.HeritageBooks.com

Published 2007 by
HERITAGE BOOKS, INC.
Publishing Division
65 East Main Street
Westminster, Maryland 21157-5026

Copyright © 2000 Richard S. Hutchinson

Other books by the author:
Abstracts of the Council of Safety Minutes, State of New Jersey, 1777-1778
Burlington County, New Jersey Deed Abstracts: Books A, B and C
Middlesex County, New Jersey Deed Abstracts: Book 1
Monmouth County, New Jersey Deeds: Books A, B, C and D
Abstracts of the Deaths and Marriages in the Hightstown Gazette *[New Jersey], 4 January 1872–27 December 1877*
Abstracts of the Deaths and Marriages in the Hightstown Gazette *[New Jersey], 3 January 1878–29 December 1881*
Abstracts of the Deaths and Marriages in the Hightstown Gazette *[New Jersey], 5 January 1882–31 December 1885*
Abstracts of the Deaths and Marriages in the Hightstown Gazette *[New Jersey], 7 January 1886–26 December 1889*
The Mercer County Genealogical Quarterly [New Jersey], Volumes 1-6
CD: The Mercer County Genealogical Quarterly [New Jersey], Volumes 1-6

All rights reserved. No part of this book may be reproduced or transmitted in any form or by any means, electronic or mechanical, including photocopying, recording or by any information storage and retrieval system without written permission from the author, except for the inclusion of brief quotations in a review.

International Standard Book Number: 978-0-7884-1661-3

Introduction

The *Hightstown Gazette*
Hightstown, New Jersey

Location

The Village of Hightstown was originally in Windsor Township, Middlesex County, New Jersey, until 1797 when the township was divided into two townships: East Windsor Township, which included the Village of Hightstown, and West Windsor Township. In 1838, Hightstown and the two above townships became part of a newly formed county, Mercer County, having been taken from a large portion of Middlesex County. Hightstown became a Borough within East Windsor Township in March 1853. Then in 1860, Washington Township was created from a large portion of East Windsor Township; again with Hightstown remaining in East Windsor Township.

Thomas F. Gordon, in his 1834 "Gazetteer of the State of New Jersey", described Hightstown, as follows: "p-t. Of East Windsor t-ship, Middlesex co., on the turnpike road from Bordentown to Cranberry, and on Rocky Brook, 13 miles from Bordentown, 183 from W.C., and 18 from Trenton; contains a Baptist and Presbyterian church, 3 taverns, 2 stores, a grist mill and saw mill, and from 30 to 40 dwellings. The rail-road from Bordentown to Amboy passes through the town, and a line of stages runs thence to Princeton, &c." In 1849, the village boosted 600 inhabitants. Today, Hightstown is centrally located on the New Jersey Turnpike (Exit 8), approximately fifteen miles east of Trenton, and equally distant from Philadelphia and New York, by fifty miles.

History of the *Hightstown Gazette*

This newspaper has had many owners and editors and has changed its name several times. The first newspaper in Hightstown, New Jersey was published on 30 June 1849 by James Yard and Jacob Stults and was called the *Village Record*. On 20 December 1849, Mr. Yard sold his interest in the paper to Edward C. Taylor, president of the Central Bank of Hightstown, citing bad health. On 9 May 1851, Mr. Stults severed his connection with the paper and the *Village Record* was published alone by Mr. Taylor until 1 January 1852, when he put the paper into the hands of Dr. B. H. Peterson, a resident physician, who changed the paper's name to the *Hightstown Gazette*. This arrangement only lasted a very short period of time, as Dr. Peterson sold it back to Mr. Taylor on 12 May 1852. On 25 June 1852, Mr. James Yard, one of the original owners of the paper who was now in better health, wanted the paper back and it was returned to him by Mr. Taylor. Mr. Yard immediately changed the paper's name back to the *Village Record* and carried on the paper under that banner until 21 January 1854, when he left the paper to become the editor of the *Monmouth Press* in Freehold, New Jersey. Mr. Yard then sold the paper back to the other original owner, Jacob Stults, and to Morgan F. Mount. Mr. Mount remained with the paper until 1 January 1855, when he sold his interest in the paper to Mr. Stults, who now became the sole proprietor of the *Village Record* newspaper.

The newspaper took a certain position and became involved in an 1857 controversy involving the Methodist and Universalist churches. The result of the paper's involvement caused a rival newspaper, the *Hightstown Excelsior*, to begin publishing in the community in opposition to the *Village Record*. However, it only lasted four years and had four editors; first C. M. Norton, then Daniel Taggart, C. W. Mount, and Mr. Norton again. At the end of those four years, which brings us to 1861, it was agreed between all parties to end the rivalry. With all parties satisfied, the *Hightstown Excelsior* and the *Village Record* agreed to merge and unite under the name of the *Hightstown Gazette* and to be run by the previous two paper's proprietors; Jacob Stults and C. M. Norton. In September 1862, Mr. Norton retired from the newspaper business and Mr. Jacob Stults, once again, became the sole proprietor of the paper known as the *Hightstown Gazette*. He ran it until April 1870, when he moved on to the *Monmouth Democrat* and turned the paper over to Rev. Thomas Baird Appleget, who became editor and proprietor. Fred Burnell Appleget was subsequently brought into the paper in April 1890, and with Thomas Appleget as the publisher, Fred B. Appleget became the editor. On 28 Feb 1904, Thomas B. Appleget died and after his death, the paper continued to be run by Fred B. Appleget as both editor and publisher.

In March 1907, after working on numerous other newspapers around the country, Jacob Stults returned to Hightstown. With Fred B. Appleget as the proprietor, once again, Jacob Stults became editor and publisher of the *Hightstown Gazette*. On 16 January 1908, Lorenzo D. Tillyer purchased the paper, Jacob Stults stayed on, and jointly, they edited the paper. This arrangement apparently ceased on 2 March 1911, when the name of Jacob Stults vanished from the masthead of the paper. [Jacob Stults died on 21 January 1916.] Tillyer continued to publish the paper until 7 November 1912, at which time he sold it to George P. Dennis, and since 1912, the paper has been owned, published and edited by the Dennis family of Hightstown, NJ. Today, in the year 2000, this paper is still being printed under the banner *Hightstown Gazette* by its feisty, but much respected lady editor, Ms. Kathyrn Dennis.

Importance of this Newspaper to Researchers

This paper was, and is, a weekly paper, published for the majority of its life every Thursday, and consisted of four pages. But, in those four pages, one can find not only the history of a community and its people but the history of the people and an entire area of a state. Most importantly, one full page was dedicated to "Local" news consisting of deaths, marriages, who was visiting whom, who was sick, moving, building a new house or business, etc.

With Hightstown less than two miles in one direction from Monmouth County and the same distance in another direction to Middlesex County, the newspaper carried a great deal of information on the people from these counties. As was the custom in those days, the editors exchanged newspapers with each other and the *Hightstown Gazette* carried those items of personal news from the exchanged papers covering other areas of the state. It also included news from other states when it reflected upon previous area residents who had migrated elsewhere.

The vast majority of the newspaper's issues have been saved and are intact, including issues of the *Village Record* and the *Hightstown Excelsior*. The largest group of papers now missing are from the Civil War years from 1862-1865 and the year 1904. All of the early Hightstown newspaper issues known to exist are in the possession of the Hightstown-East Windsor Historical Society. At this time, all known issues of the *Hightstown Gazette* have now been microfilmed up through 1964. Presently (July 2000), the Society has obtained grant funding and is in the process of completing the filming the paper's issues from 1965 through 1999.

Previous Abstracts

Both the marriages and deaths from the early issues of the *Village Record* and the *Hightstown Gazette*, from 30 July 1849 through 27 November 1862, were extracted in 1987 by Patricia Davison Ely, of Neptune, New Jersey and were published and sold privately. Both of these works are in the Library of the Hightstown-East Windsor Historical Society.

The Present Volume of Abstracts

This series of the abstracts overlaps Mrs. Ely's previous work by several months but I believed it to be important to begin these abstracts of the *Hightstown Gazette* with the first issue of the paper under that banner. Therefore, this first volume of abstracts begins on 10 April 1861 and runs through 28 December 1871; minus the missing Civil War years of November 1862 through September 1865.

These abstracts list the deaths of ALL persons, as reported by the newspaper, who died in New Jersey or those who had "roots" to New Jersey. They DO NOT include the deaths of people who died in other states that were simply reported on the national page of the paper. The abstracts are listed by three categories: the date of the paper, the abstracted item, and a code letter; "D" for death or "M" for marriage. The date of the paper is listed by six digits and the dates are listed in ascending order. The first two digits represents the year, the second two represents the month and the third two represents the day. For example, the date "700101" would be 1870 January 1; "721223" would be 1872 December 23, etc.

The abstracts were taken from the paper's microfilm but there were many times when the microfilm could not be read due to blurred paper ink, clogged type, darkness of the newspaper due to water stains, tears in the paper, bad microfilm, etc. Having said this, over ninety-nine percent of the deaths and marriages have been accurately abstracted. And, when there was still a question regarding the items that could be read and abstracted, they were checked against the original papers. However, with any type research using these types of research tools, you should always consult the original document whenever possible to insure the accuracy of the item.

The Hightstown-East Windsor Historical Society will conduct a limited search of the original issues, if you do not see an abstracted item for a death or marriage that you know occurred in the Hightstown-East Windsor Township area on a specific date. However, be aware that in all newspapers, not every event was reported. Likewise, if you find an abstract you are interested in and want a copy of the complete article, they will copy the original item as found in the original newspaper. Both of these services will be completed for a reasonable fee plus postage and handling. All requests for such services must be in writing and should be addressed to the attention of the Library Committee, Hightstown-East Windsor Historical Society, 164 North Main St, Hightstown, New Jersey 08520.

I would like to thank the East Windsor Historical Society for allowing access to the newspaper's microfilm for this project, to John Orr for answering my questions, but most importantly I want to thank Kate Middleton, Society Librarian, for answering my many requests when questions arose on this project.

Abstracts of the Deaths and Marriages in the *Hightstown Gazette*, 18 April 1861 - 28 December 1871

****

610418	On the 4th inst., by Rev. L. Smith, James C. Norris to Mrs. Matilda Hutchinson, daughter of the late Thomas Ely, all of this place. , M
610418	On the 7th inst., by Rev. L. Smith, Reuben Riggs to Miss Elizabeth Reed, of Hightstown. , M
610516	On Friday last, the body of Mr. John Clark, residing on the Freehold road, a few miles from the borough, was found suspended from the rafter of his barn. , D
610523	By Rev. R. Taylor, on the 13th ult., David Evans and Miss Margaret M. Smith, both of Englishtown. , M
610523	Died - On Tuesday, the 21st., John E. Perrine, near Cranbury, aged 45. , D
610530	At the residence of the bride, on the 22nd inst., by Rev. Milton Relyea, Richard Bampton to Miss Sarah A. E. Mills, both of Windsor. , M
610530	In Bordentown, on the 5th inst., Aaron Robbins, formerly of Cranbury, aged 45 years. , D
610627	In this borough on the 24th inst., Alsena E., daughter of John C. and Margaret Johnson, aged 13 months and 13 days. , D
610704	On Tuesday of last week, a farmer, Alfred Clayton, residing at Prospect Plains, committed suicide by hanging in his barn. He leaves a wife and child. , D
610704	Three boys were drowned a few days ago at Green's Pond near Long Branch. There were the sons of John McIntire, Michael Maps, and George Waters, and were from 14 to 16 years of age. , D
610711	In this borough, on Tuesday, the 9th inst., by Rev. R. Taylor, George W. Coward to Miss M. Louise Pritchard, daughter of Dr. Pritchard, all of Hightstown. , M
610711	On the railroad between Bordentown and White Hill, Clayton Palmer, about 80, better known as "The Birch Broom Man", was struck by a train and killed. He made his living by making and selling birch brooms. , D

Abstracts of the Deaths and Marriages in the *Hightstown Gazette*, 18 April 1861 - 28 December 1871

****

610718	July 4th, by Rev. L. Smith, Augustus Van Nosten, of Dutch Neck, to Miss Rachel Ann Green, of this place. , M
610718	Mr. Edward Tunis was drowned at Imlaystown, Monmouth county on Monday while bathing. He was holding on to the sides of a boat but it was leaking so badly it sank. He could not swim. , D
610725	Charles Brandt, son of Richard Brandt, Hatter, of Trenton, was among those killed in the recent battle in Virginia. He was a member of the 71st Reg, of New York. , D
610725	Joseph B. Webster, fell dead on Saturday, while working on the farm of Wm. N. Stults, near Cranbury. , D
610725	On Saturday, the 13th, at Wyckoff Mills, the son of John Wolf, aged 10, drowned after falling in while fishing. , D
610725	William Price, member of the Legislature from Sussex county, died on the 13th inst. after a long illness. , D
610801	Among the killed at Bull Run, was a young man named Uselma Duncan, son of the widow Duncan of Princeton. He belonged to the New York 71st Reg. , D
610801	At Manchester, Mass., on the 26th inst., after a protracted illness, Miss Barker, for some time a Teacher in this place. , D
610801	On Wednesday, the 7th inst., infant daughter of Daniel W. and Mary E. Perrine, aged 5 months and 2 days. Funeral in this Borough this (Thursday) morning. , D
610808	Among those slain in the recent battle was James Smith, formerly of Freehold. , D
610822	At Cranberry, on the 6th inst., by Rev. Thomas D. Hoover, Rev. John Lowrey to Miss Lydia Clarke of Cranberry. , M
610822	At Hoboken on the 5th inst., by the Rev. Alfred Harris, Robert Stewart of South Amboy to Miss Maggie Thompson of Leedsville. , M
610822	By Rev. R. Taylor, on the 10th inst., Jonathan Robbins and Miss Delia Cosh, both of Jamesburg. , M

Abstracts of the Deaths and Marriages in the *Hightstown Gazette*, 18 April 1861 - 28 December 1871

****

610822	On the 11th inst., of cholera infantum, infant daughter of Lemuel Williamson, aged 1 year. , D
610822	On the 17th inst., of whooping cough, infant daughter of Wm. Courtney, aged 8 months. , D
610822	On the 18th inst., at Windsor, Eli Updyke, in the 76th year of his age. , D
610822	On the 18th inst., of cholera infantum, child of James Doley, aged 9 months. , D
610822	On the 8th inst., of cholera infantum infant daughter of William Walton, aged 1 year. , D
610822	On the 8th inst., of whooping cough, infant daughter of Stephen Courtney, aged 4 years. , D
610829	On Saturday, 17th inst., at Arrowsmith's Mills, near Keyport, during a drunken brawl, a Frenchman formerly of NY, was shot dead by a man named Job Smith. , D
610829	On the 13th inst., of Dropsy, Sarah E. Gravatt, aged 62 years. , D
610829	On Wednesday, the 10th ult., at the residence of her daughter in this place, Mrs. Mercy Mount, in the 84th year of her age. , D
610905	On the 23rd ult., of whooping cough, Emma, daughter of Reuben Norris, aged 9 months and 2 days. , D
610905	On Tuesday, the 3rd inst., after a painful illness, Freeman R. Pullen, aged 36 years and 2 months. , D
610912	Died - On Tuesday, the 10th inst., at Manalapan, Joseph Reed. , D
610912	Wm. Lawson of Newark, who was wounded in the War died from his injuries. Another who died in the skirmish was Corporal Hand of Plainfield, who leaves a wife and two children. , D
610919	On Monday, the 16th inst., infant daughter of Daniel W. Perrine, aged 6 months and 2 weeks. , D

Abstracts of the Deaths and Marriages in the *Hightstown Gazette*, 18 April 1861 - 28 December 1871
****

610919	On Saturday, the 14th, the wife of James Conover, aged 77 years. , D
610926	On the 3rd by Rev. M. Relyea, George Stelle to Jane A. Brown, both of Windsor. , M
610926	On the 4th by Rev. M. Relyea, at Windsor, John M. Malsbury to Ellen Peer. , M
611003	In Trenton, on the 30th ult., Sarah A., wife of Samuel S. Hill, formerly of this place. , D
611003	Near Harmony, in Middletown township, Monmouth county last week, a boy named Thomas Greely was killed when he jumped off of a moving wagon. , D
611024	After a skirmish with the enemy on Friday last, a man named Silvers of near Princeton was killed. He belonged to Co, A, 1st Reg., NJ Vols. , D
611031	At Edinburgh, Mercer county, NJ, on the 23rd inst., by Rev. A. L. Armstrong of Dutch Neck, William Clark of Princeton to Miss Emily B. Hill, daughter of David Hill of Edinburgh. , M
611031	Clayton Taylor of New Egypt met his death on Sunday, October 13th, in a gunning accident in which his gun was accidently discharged by his dog. He was married. , D
611107	Sigismund Fellner, of a Jewish family in Mainze, Grand Duchy of Hesse Darmstadt, Germany, who arrived in this country a few days since on the 'Bavaria, and who took lodgings in New York, was found dead in Middletown, NJ. , D
611114	On the 6th inst., Mary, daughter of Patrick Dolan, aged 3 years and 6 months. , D
611114	Wm. Gilbert, a farmer of South Brunswick township, Middlesex county, was shot and killed by the accidental discharge of a companion's gun. , D
611121	At her residence in Crosswicks, on the 12th inst., of paralysis, Hannah Hendrickson, relict of David Hendrickson of Upper Freehold, in her 79th year. She lived the life of a widow for more than 35 years. She was devoted to her children and was a member , D
611121	At Imlaystown of the 6th inst., Martin Embley, aged 29 years. , D

Abstracts of the Deaths and Marriages in the *Hightstown Gazette*, 18 April 1861 - 28 December 1871

****

611121	Four children of James and Mahala Mount of near, have died of diphtheria within two weeks. They were aged 15, 6, and 4 years, and 20 months. , D
611121	In Freehold on the 8th inst. of consumption, John C. S. Connolly, former Editor of the "Monmouth Weekly Herald", aged 32 years. , D
611121	On the 10th inst., at Perrineville, Henry P. Thomason of consumption, aged 22 years. , D
611121	On the 13th, by Rev. T. R. Taylor, D. Augustus Vanderveer of Freehold to Miss Georgiana Hunt of Manalapan. , M
611121	On Tuesday, the 12th inst., by Rev. W. W. McMichael, Holmes W. Murphy, of Freehold to Lavinia C. Swift, of Fulton, Pa. , M
611128	At Fresh Pond, on the 14th inst., Emma, daughter of Benjamin and Emeline Budd, aged 12 years and 6 months. , D
611128	In this borough, Monday the 25th of diphtheria, James, son of Richard and Mary Barker, aged 2 years and 2 months. , D
611128	On the 13th inst., by Rev. R. Taylor, Augustus Justice to Miss Mariah Patterson, both of Milford. , M
611205	On Saturday, the 30th ult., at the residence of his brother in this borough, John H. Scattergood, of paralysis in the 60th year of his age. , D
611205	On Tuesday, the 3rd inst., of dropsy, John Applegate, aged 45 years. , D
611205	On Wednesday, the 20th ult., by Rev. Thos. D. Hoover, Vincent Perrine and Miss Sarah D. Dye, both of Middlesex county. , M
611205	On Wednesday, the 27th ult., by Rev. Thos. D. Hoover, at Cross Roads, J. Calvin Vanderveer and Miss Maria D. Schenck, both of Middlesex county. , M
611212	Near Windsor, on the 5th inst., by Rev. H. Perkins, Daniel Brown to Miss Anna Applegate. , M
611212	On Monday, the 9th inst., of disease of the heart, Mary Jewell, aged 75. , D

Abstracts of the Deaths and Marriages in the *Hightstown Gazette*, 18 April 1861 - 28 December 1871

****

611212	On Wednesday, the 4th inst., by Rev. L. Smith, Levi Solomon of Monmouth county and Miss Ellen Ely of this place. , M
611219	At the M.E. church in this borough, on Wednesday, 18th inst., by Rev. I. Winner, William S. Ayres and Miss Carrie R. Hutchinson, all of this place. , M
611219	On the 11th inst., by Rev. L. Smith, Theodore Anderson to Miss Sarah M. Chamberlain. , M
611219	On the 12th inst., by Rev. L. Smith, John R. Paxton of Jamesburg to Miss Leititia Jolly, of Spotswood. , M
611219	On the 12th inst., by Rev. L. Smith, William H. Petty to Miss Charlotte M. Jolly, both of Spotswood. , M
611226	By the Rev. A. L. Armstrong of Dutch Neck on the 18th inst., Mr. David D. Grover to Amanda, daughter of Isaac Rossell, all of West Windsor. , M
611226	By the Rev. A. L. Armstrong of Dutch Neck on the 18th inst., Mr. Voorhees K. Hutchinson of Black's Mills to Miss Eleanor K. daughter of Sylvanus Grover of South Brunswick. , M
611226	George A. Vroom, Middlesex County Clerk, died and his position is being filled. , D
611226	John Simmonds was acquitted for the murder of "young Walling at Keyport" some five weeks since. The jury ruled justifiable homicide". , D
611226	On Sunday, the 22nd inst., Mary Moore, relict of Henry A. Moore, in the 66th year of her age. , D
611226	On the 22nd inst., of diphtheria, Rachel A. Wilson, daughter of Peter E. Wilson of this place, aged 5 years, 7 months and 10 days. , D
620109	At Cranberry, on the 1st inst., by Rev. Thos D. Hoover, Wm. P. Dye to Miss Harriet Dye, both of Cranbury. , M
620109	At Cranberry, on the 2nd inst., by Rev. Thos D. Hoover, Isaiah D. Barclay to Miss Elizabeth S. Silvers, both of Middlesex County. , M

Abstracts of the Deaths and Marriages in the *Hightstown Gazette*, 18 April 1861 - 28 December 1871

****

620109	At Imlaystown, Sept 7th, by Rev. Charles M. Deitz, Joseph W. Patterson of Hightstown to Miss Elmira Burke, of Millstone township. , M
620109	At Trenton, on the 31st ult., by Mayor McKean, Jonathan S. Perrine of Perrineville, to Anna M. Kirby, of Cream Ridge. , M
620109	In this borough, Thursday, the 2nd inst., by Rev. I. Smith, Ezekiel Hulet of Springfield, Ill., to Miss Rachel Hulet, of this place. , M
620109	Near this borough, on the 7th inst., Mrs. Margaret Cook, relict of Gen. James Cook, in the 81st year of her age. , D
620109	On the 18th inst., by Rev. Charles M. Deitz, Spafford W. Dey of Hightstown to Miss Sarah R. Miller, of Imlaystown. , M
620109	On the 18th ult. by Rev. Jos. G. Symmes, Alfred Chamberlain to Miss Catherine, daughter of the late John S. Pierson. , M
620109	On the 19th ult. by Rev. Jos. G. Symmes, George S. Dey to Miss M. Augusta, daughter of Wm. D. Davison. , M
620109	On the 22nd ult., by Rev. Charles M. Deitz, Sidney W. Williams to Miss Annie Robbins, all of Imlaystown. , M
620109	On the 26th ult. by Rev. Jos. G. Symmes, William Duncan to Miss Mary Virginia, daughter of Wm. Ruding. , M
620109	On the 25th ult., of consumption, Derrick G. Dey, aged 35 years and 8 months. , D
620109	On the 30th ult., by Rev. Charles M. Deitz, Franklin M. Harker to Miss Mary R. Liming, all of Imlaystown. , M
620109	On the 3rd ult. by Rev. Jos. G. Symmes, Britton Mount to Miss Mary A., daughter of Matthias M. Perrine. , M
620116	By Rev. Thos. D. Hoover, near Prospect Plains, on the 7th inst., George Henry Davis and Miss Charlotte Hoffman, both of Middlesex County. , M

Abstracts of the Deaths and Marriages in the *Hightstown Gazette*, 18 April 1861 - 28 December 1871

****

620116	On the 15th inst., by Rev. I. Smith, Cornelius B. Stults of Cranberry, to Miss Amanda, daughter of Clark H. Silvers, Esq., of this place. , M
620116	On the 8th inst., by Rev. I. Smith, George H. Cox, of Baker's Basin, to Miss Caroline Embley, youngest daughter of Joseph Embley, Esq. , M
620123	On Friday, the 17th inst., in this borough, Thomas Tulley, aged 63 years, a native of Ireland. , D
620130	By the Rev. Thos. D. Hoover, at Plainsborough on the 15th inst., Symmes H. Wiley to Miss Ann F. Cox, both of Middlesex County. , M
620130	On the 15th inst., by Rev. J. G. Symmes, Elias D. Applegate to Miss Maria M., daughter of Peter D. Hibbetts. , M
620130	On the 1st inst., by Rev. J. G. Symmes, Elias Brown to Miss Sarah I., daughter of John E. Perrine, dec'd. , M
620130	On the 7th inst., by Rev. J. G. Symmes, Wm. Reed Scelover to Miss Susan C., daughter of Geo. T. McDowell, dec'd. , M
620130	On the 8th inst., by Rev. J. G. Symmes, Samuel Ely Perrine to Miss Catharine V., daughter of Alex. C. Snedeker. , M
620130	On Thursday, the 23rd inst., of consumption, Henry Vaughn, aged 30 years, 10 months and 6 days. , D
620206	At Windsor, on the 3rd inst., Annie, wife of Robert Haborn, aged about 26. , D
620206	At Windsor, on Tuesday, the 4th inst., Sarah Perrine, relict of Maj. John Perrine of Manalapan, in the 77th year of her age. Funeral from the First Presbyterian Church of Millstone, Monmouth County, on Sat., the 8th inst. , D
620206	In Trenton, on the 3rd inst., Mary H., wife of John Disborough, in the 63rd year of her age. Interment at Perrineville. , D
620206	On Friday, the 31st ult, Mary, wife of Israel Pearce, of cancer, in the 56th year of her age. , D

Abstracts of the Deaths and Marriages in the *Hightstown Gazette*, 18 April 1861 - 28 December 1871

****

620206	On the 2nd inst., of consumption, Enoch Mount, aged 46 years, 7 months, 23 days. , D
620206	On the 30th, by Rev. A. L. Armstrong, of Dutch Neck, at the residence of David Stonaker, Henry E. Harle of Princeton Basin to Miss Rebecca Stonaker of Penn's Neck. , M
620206	On the 5th inst., of membranes croup, youngest child of J. L. Snyder, aged 20 months. , D
620213	At Prospect Plains, by Rev. Thos. D. Hoover, on the 6th inst., Arthur V. Stults to Miss Elizabeth Ann, daughter of John Covert. , M
620220	On Saturday, the 15th inst., Ezekiel Dey, aged 94 years all to 5 days. , D
620227	On the 15th inst., by Rev. L. Smith, John M. Cox of Plainsborough to Miss Ann Augusta Thompson of Monroe. , M
620227	On Tuesday, the 25th inst., infant son of Dermond Somers, aged 3 years. , D
620227	On Tuesday, the body of Orville Babcock, a teacher, was found in the apple orchard of Jesse Embley, near Bergen's Mills. A bruise was discovered on his head and it is believed that he hit his head, was stunned, and died due to exposure. , D
620313	In Cranberry, on the 21st ult., Isaac G. Snedeker, aged 80 years. , D
620313	On March 10th, by Rev. L. Smith, Theodore Lamberson of Middletown Point, to Miss Kate A. Vaughan, of Dutch Neck. , M
620313	Rev. J. L Lenhart, Chaplain on board the "Cumberland", and who is supposedly drowned, was a resident of Newark. , D
620320	On the 6th, by Rev. M. Relyeu of Windsor, James Carson to Miss Mary E. Moore, both of Allentown, NJ. , M
620320	On this Thursday morning, of scarlet fever, James, son of Dr. L. and Caroline Wilbur, aged 3 years and 11 months. , D

Abstracts of the Deaths and Marriages in the *Hightstown Gazette*, 18 April 1861 - 28 December 1871

****

620403	At Camp Baker, Lower Potomac, Md., on the 20th ult., James P. Holeman, of typhoid fever, aged 19 years, a member of Co. A., 6th Reg, NJ Vols. , D
620403	On Monday, the 31st ult., of croup, Lilly Irene, daughter of James C. and Matilda Norris, aged 10 weeks. , D
620410	Harriet M., wife of Com. R. F. Stockton of Princeton, died in Philadelphia on the 1st inst., and was buried on Thursday in the Princeton Cemetery. , D
620410	Near Bergen's Mills on the 4th inst., child of Cornelius Rue, aged 11 years. , D
620410	On Sunday the 6th inst., near this borough, Alfred Pullen. , D
620410	On the 28th ult., of dropsy, daughter of Tobias Compton, aged 18 months. , D
620410	On the 3rd inst., child of Aaron Hulse, aged 4 years. , D
620410	On the 3rd inst., near Windsor, Mrs. Jobs, aged about 70. , D
620417	Hon. Theodore Frelinghuysen died at his residence in New Brunswick, on Saturday, the 12th inst., after a lingering illness. He was 75 years old, born in Millstone, Somerset Co, 28 Mar 1787. His father was a lawyer and took part in the battles of Trenton and Monmouth in the Revolution and holds the distinction of having shot the Hessian commander, Rahl. [Long article on his career.] , D
620417	Near Bergen's Mills, on the 4th inst., child of Cornelius Rue, aged 11 years, of scarlet fever. , D
620417	Near Bergen's Mills, on the 4th inst., child of Cornelius Rue, aged 4 years, of scarlet fever. , D
620424	At Windsor, NJ, April 23rd, Barclay Perrine. Funeral from his late residence, Saturday, April 26th. , D
620424	Hon. Joseph W. Pharo, late Senator from Burlington county, died on Wed., the 16th inst., at his residence in Tuckerton. He was 49 years old. , D
620424	On the 16th inst., by Rev. O. T. Walker, Samuel S. Hill to Miss Sarah B. Mott, all of Trenton. , M

Abstracts of the Deaths and Marriages in the *Hightstown Gazette*, 18 April 1861 - 28 December 1871

****

620501	At Newborne, N.C., on the 10th ult., of typhoid fever, Alfred Perrine of Co. M, 9th Reg., NJ Vols., son of Henry Perrine, near Cranberry. , D
620501	Near Cranberry, on the 23rd ult., of croup, Mary Anna, daughter of G. W. and Matilda Grant, aged 5 years. , D
620508	On the 3rd inst., of croup, only child of Anthony Coleman, aged 3 months. , D
620508	On the 4th inst., Charles, oldest son of Daniel Johnes, aged 16 years. , D
620515	In West Windsor, on the 11th inst., Sarah Cox, a slave, aged 93 years. , D
620515	Killed in the battle of Williamsburgh, VA, James M. Evernham, Hightstown, shot through the head; James Carr of near Hightstown, killed, shot through the breast; Jos. S. Price, Trenton, shot through the head; Peter A. Jimeson, of Ocean County. , D
620515	Near Half Acre, on the 9th inst., John Thompson. , D
620522	At Trenton, on Tuesday, the 20th inst., of heart disease, James T. Sherman, for many years editor of the "state Gazette", aged 47 years. , D
620529	A child of Ezckiel Hughes died as the result of being given laudanum which had been given in error by the clerk in Mr. Holcomb's drugstore. The clerk was distracted as he was reaching for the bottle of Godfrey's Cordial and picked the laudanum bottle by mistake as both bottles sat on the shelf next to each other. , D
620529	May 26th, by Rev. L. Smith, Maj. E. T. R. Applegate, of Milford, to Miss Lavinia, daughter of the late Thomas Ely, Esq. , M
620612	Alfred Blake of the 5th NJ Reg., wounded in the arm and then attacked by fever, died on the 26th ult. , D
620612	Killed in War from area - Sgt. Robbins, James Reamer, Wm. Hillyer, Gilbert Hartman, Stephen Burns, Joseph M. Moore. , D
620612	On Sunday, the 8th inst., of consumption, Richard Applegate, aged 32. , D

Abstracts of the Deaths and Marriages in the *Hightstown Gazette*, 18 April 1861 - 28 December 1871

****

620612	This morning, June 12th, by Rev. Abel C. Thomas, Isaac Keeler of Philadelphia to Miss Cordella Pullen, daughter of Isaac Pullen, of this place. , M
620710	At James River Hospital, Va., May 25th, of a wound received in the battle of Williamsburg, Charles Lehming, of this place. , D
620710	Capt Dodd, of the 17th Inf., son of Rev. Dodd of Princeton, was killed in battle; also Maj. N.B. Rossell (who belonged to Trenton) of the 3rd Infantry died. , D
620710	In Hightstown on the 6th inst., by Rev. H.M. Brown, Robert A.G. Daymond, Esq. of Trenton to Caroline A. Edwards, of this place. , M
620724	On Friday, 18th inst., after a lingering illness, William Johnes Smith, oldest son of Col. R. M. Smith, in the 27th year of his age. , D
620724	On Tuesday, 22nd inst., at the residence of her father, Enos Ayres, Helen, wife of George Fisher, of consumption. , D
620731	A man named David Anderson of Pennington, attempted to jump onto a moving train but fell under the wheels crushing his leg. He lost so much blood that he died. , D
620731	On Friday, 18th inst., after a lingering illness, William Johnes Smith, eldest son of Col. R. M. Smith, in the 27th year of his age. , D
620731	On Monday, Joseph Winfield, only child of Joseph and Alice McMurran, aged 11 months. , D
620731	On the 20th ult., of whooping cough, only child of William A. Potts, aged 7 weeks. , D
620814	At the M.E. parsonage, in this place, on the 7th inst., by Rev. H.M. Brown, Edward T. Lane of Bordentown to Rebecca Atkinson of New Egypt, NJ. , M
620821	At the Quartermaster's Hospital, Washington, DC, on the 17th inst., of typhoid fever, Lewis Perrine, aged 20. , D

Abstracts of the Deaths and Marriages in the *Hightstown Gazette*, 18 April 1861 - 28 December 1871

****

620821	Lieut. Charles S. Allen, of the Governor's Guard, of Princeton, died on Friday last. His funeral on Monday was attended by many citizens and the Borough Council, of which he was a member. Mr. Allen was a young man. , D
620821	On the 14th inst., by Rev. H.M. Brown, Samuel Hicks to Elizabeth Debow, all of this place. , M
620911	At Milford of the 1st inst., of diphtheria, Henry, son of John Maple, aged 8 years. , D
620911	At South Amboy week before last, Jackson Bloodgood was killed by Adolf Kunzick, a keeper of a beer saloon, after Bloodgood became drunk and was threatening to kill another patron named Kunzick. , D
620911	Capt. E.A. Acton, formerly of Salem, was killed in the late Bull Run fight. , D
620911	Maj. Gen. Phillip Kearney, born June 2, 1815, of Irish descent, his g-g-grandfather having settled in Monmouth county in 1716, died in a recent battle. His body was conveyed to his home in Newark, NJ on Friday last. [Long article on his career.] , D
620911	On the 14th ult., by Rev. F. Robbins, Jessee Green to Mary English of this place. , M
620911	On the 2nd ult., at Windsor, Clifford Baldwin, only child of Rev. M. Relyea, aged 4 months. , D
620911	On the 31st ult., child of George S. H. Applegate, aged 3 months. , D
620911	On the 8th inst., of dysentery, child of John Holmes, aged 18 months. , D
620911	The body of Gen. George W. Taylor, who died form a wound received in the late battles, has been brought to the residence of friends near Clinton, Hunterdon Co. He was between 50 and 60 years old. A son and nephew, both bearing the same name were also wounded in the same engagement. [Article has more info on his career.] , D

Abstracts of the Deaths and Marriages in the *Hightstown Gazette*, 18 April 1861 - 28 December 1871

620918	Frederick W. Sovereign, 21, of the 5th Reg., NY Vols., only son of Rev. Thomas Sovereign, of the NJ Methodist Conference, was killed at the battle of Bull Run, Aug. 30th., D
620918	Senator Thompson died at his residence in Princeton on Friday, the 12th inst. of a lingering sickness., D
620925	Capt. John Ditmars of Newark was killed in a battle on Wednesday., D
620925	Killed in the 13th NJ Reg - Jesse R. Cole, Calvin Armstrong, Corp. Brant., D
620925	On Saturday, 20th inst., of Diphtheria, Louise, oldest child of Wicoff and Frances Norton, aged 7 years and 6 months., D
621016	Near this place on Saturday last, Mary, daughter of James Donnel, aged 5 years., D
621023	John Butcher, Esq., formerly of this borough, died in Brooklyn, on Thursday last. He was a Justice of Peace and also Mayor of this borough. His funeral took place at Hamilton Square., D
621120	At Perrineville, on the 5th inst., of consumption, Rebecca, wife of Ezekiel Davison, aged 50 years., D
621120	At Toms River of Tuesday, the 28th ult., James B. Lane, Esq., in the 77th year of his age. He was a one time post master at Tom's River and contributed to the press in the states of New Jersey and New York, D
621120	Henry Pierce, of Long Branch, accidently shot himself and died., D
621120	J. Rowland, a jeweler of Princeton, was murdered on Thursday evening after having been struck over the head. The suspect, a man named Lewis, was arrested., D
621120	On Nov 8th, at the house of the bride's father, by Rev. C. F. Worrell, C. N. Silvers, son of Nelson Silvers, Esq., of Millstone to Miss Elmira, daughter of J. B. Stillwell of Millstone., M

Abstracts of the Deaths and Marriages in the *Hightstown Gazette*, 18 April 1861 - 28 December 1871

****

650907	Memoriam - Joseph M. McChesney, aged 27 died from wound received during the War. In July 1864, he married Miss Lizzie McChesney of Middletown Point. He was buried beneath the family monument at Cranberry, NJ. , D, M
650907	On Saturday last, the daughter of James Scott, aged about 14, and residing near this place, died as the result of her injuries from being severely burned after attempting to fill a burning lamp with kerosene. , D
650914	Hon. Lyman A. Chandler, for the last 3 years State Senator from Morris County, died at his residence in Rockaway on the 11th inst. , D
650914	In St. Mark's church, Newark, NY[NJ?], on the 5th inst., by the Rev. P. Teller Babbitt, Ellery C. Redfield, of Clifton Springs, NY, to Miss Josephine M.L. Brownell, of the first mentioned place. , M
650914	On the 5th inst., at the residence of the bride's father, by Rev. A. L. Armstrong, of Dutch Neck, Rev. P.B. Van Syckel, of the Presbyterian church of Columbus, NJ to Miss Rebecca E. Rue, daughter of Enoch Rue of Dutch Neck, NJ. , M
650928	At Clarksburg, on Sunday last, 24th inst., of typhoid fever, Maria, wife of Amos Tantum, aged 22 years. , D
650928	At Windsor, Sept 16th, by Randal C. Robbins, Justice of the Peace, Thomas Hendrickson to Miss Adelaide Cook, both of Bordentown. , M
650928	Near Hightstown on the 9th inst., of diphtheria, Charles, aged 9 years, and on the 16th, Ruliff H., aged 4 years, children of Daniel Pippenger. , D
650928	Newtown - Sarah Cheeseman, without just cause, has left my bed and board ... and I shall pay no debts of her contracting. Signed - Henry Cheeseman. , M
651005	In this borough, on Thursday, Sept 21st, of congestion of the lungs, Anna Munro, youngest child of Samuel and Ella W. Holcombe. Remains were taken to New Brunswick for interment. , D
651005	Near this place, on the 23rd ult., of consumption, John V. Anderson, aged 67 years. , D

Abstracts of the Deaths and Marriages in the *Hightstown Gazette*, 18 April 1861 - 28 December 1871

****

651005	On the 30th of September, by Rev. S.E. Post, Charles Wilson to Miss Jane A. Williams, both of Hightstown. , M
651012	Near Bergen's Mills, of the 30th ult., of dysentery, Daniel Johnes Rue, aged 53 years. , D
651012	Near Bergen's Mills, on the 28th ult., Harvey P., son of Samuel Rue, aged 9 months. , D
651012	Near Bergen's Mills, Sept 23d, of diphtheria, Adelia, daughter of Daniel Pittenger, aged one year four months. , D
651012	Near Locust Corner on the 3d inst., James W., son of Alfred Stevenson, aged 8 months. , D
651012	Near Red Tavern, on the 28th ult., of diphtheria, Emma, aged 9 years, and on the 8th inst., of the same disease, Catharine, aged 7 years, children of Wm. Mount. , D
651012	On Wednesday, September 27th, Mrs. Virginia Ruding of Cranberry died. She was born in Lyons, France in 1790 and came to America in 1832. , D
651012	Richard Barker, son of once Rev. E. B. Barker of the Baptist Church of Hightstown died at Natchez, Miss., Sept 14, 1865 of typhoid fever, leaving a wife and two sons. The youngest son died Nov 25, 1861. He was married to Mary E. Chamberlain, a member of Hightstown Baptist Church, by his father, on 10 December 1845. He enlisted in the 2nd. NJ Calvary in September 1863. , D
651019	In this borough, on the 16th inst., William B., son of James B. Richardson, aged 24 years. , D
651019	On Sunday, the 1st inst., Rev. Oliver Badgeley, of the Newark Conference, died suddenly in a field near his home. His daughter found him but he was unable to speak and soon died. He had been in the ministry for over 30 years. His funeral took place in Belvedere, NJ. , D
651026	Officer McWilliams, a Jersey City detective, shot and killed a notorious rowdy, John Johnson, on Saturday in Courtlandt street, near West. , D

Abstracts of the Deaths and Marriages in the *Hightstown Gazette*, 18 April 1861 - 28 December 1871

****

651026	Rev. Thomas Roberts, one of the old Baptist ministers of NJ, died recently at the residence of his son, Daniel Roberts, near Leonardsville. , D
651026	Mercer Cemetery. He was killed by a rebel bullet in a skirmish at Fisher's Hill on the 8th of October in 1864. He was buried by the 18th PA Cavalry on a farm of a Union man. , D
651102	At the home of the bride in this Borough on Thursday, 26th ult., by Rev. S. S. Shriver, assisted by Rev. John McCluskey, the Rev. James M. Maxwell, pastor of the Twelfth Presbyterian church of Baltimore, Md, to Miss Gertrude A. Appleget. , M
651102	In the Baptist parsonage, Freehold, on the 12th inst., by Rev. D.S. Parmelee, Jonathan F. Reed, of Millstone to Miss Melissa Vancleaf, of Hightstown. , M
651102	On the 12th inst., at the residence of John Thompson, Esq., Pa., by the Rev. D. R. Fraser, Charles D. Hendrickson of Monmouth county, NJ, to Lizzie M., daughter of the late George Rue of Cranberry, NJ. , M
651102	On the 26th ult., in this borough, Mrs. Mary H. Rofers, aged 88 years, 5 months, 20 days. , D
651109	A man named Perrine was murdered at Freehold on Friday last. , D
651109	On Wednesday, Patrick McDonald, about 20 years, due to gangrene resulted from injuries after falling form a coal train and his legs being crushed. He was from Bordentown and was buried there. He served over 3 years in the Army, was wounded at Roanoke, captured and held prisoner for 11 months. , D
651116	Benjamin F. Yard, late Assistant Surgeon of the 14th NJ Vols, died at his residence near Pennington, on the 10th inst., in the 49th year of his age. , D
651116	In the morning hours of Saturday last in Freehold, D.C. Perrine of Brocket's Mills, near Englishtown, was found dying from knife wounds inflicted by 4 or 5 men. He died later in the morning., D

Abstracts of the Deaths and Marriages in the *Hightstown Gazette*, 18 April 1861 - 28 December 1871

****

651123	In Cranberry, at the parsonage, by Rev. T.D. Hoover, on the 26th of Oct, of the Second Church, Morgan Wilson and Adelaide Ayres, both of Mercer county, NJ. , M
651123	In this borough, Nov 16, of consumption, Jane L., wife of Charles L. Robbins, ged 40 years. , D
651123	Jerry Lalor, residing near Trenton, drove into the canal at Lamberton and was drowned. , D
651123	The funeral of Henry L. Gordon, proprietor of the Williard's Hotel at Washington, who was killed in a railroad accident at Newark, NJ, was attended at Holderness, N.H. on Sunday. , D
651130	In Cecil County, Maryland, on the 6th inst., of congestion of the brain, Henry C. Roman, aged about 27 years. , D
651130	On November 23, 1864, Peter J. Cueuel, of Morristown, murdered his wife. He was tried, convicted and sentenced to death which was carried out in the jail yard in Morristown on Friday, the 24th inst. His children visited him the night before, but two of them returned to see him before the execution. , D
651207	December 6th, by Rev. S.E. Post, John W. Sanford of Farmingdale, Monmouth county, to Miss Mary F., daughter of Joseph H. Jimeson, Esq., of this borough. , M
651207	On the 25th ult., of inflammation of the lungs, Addison Chamberlain, son of Joseph Chamberlain, aged 3 months. , D
651214	At Hightstown, on the 6th inst., by Rev. I. Butterfield, John G. Wright of East Windsor and Miss Anna M. Coward of the same place. , M
651214	At the residence of the bride's father, in South Brunswick, by Rev. I. Butterfield, on the 6th inst., R. Baxter Conover, of Monroe to Miss Sarah B., daughter of T. Salter Snedeker, Esq. , M
651214	At Windsor on the 3rd inst., of consumption, John, son of Melville Saley, aged 4 months. , D

Abstracts of the Deaths and Marriages in the *Hightstown Gazette*, 18 April 1861 - 28 December 1871

****

651214	By Rev. A.K. Street, in Burlington, NJ, Edward Mills of Camden to Miss Sallie Irene, daughter of the officiating minister. , M
651214	On Nov 15th, by Rev K.P. Ketchum, George D. Coward to Miss Louisa S. Burtis, both of Allentown. , M
651214	Two deaths due to violence occurred in Trenton during the past week. On Friday night, Jacob Skillman had a fight with Chas. G. Updike and knocked him down where he hit his head and died from the injuries. On Saturday, James Bamford was also badly beaten by two soldiers that he died on Monday. , D
651221	A day or two since, a man named John S. Hand, who lived in Tuckahoe, NJ was instantly killed when his gun accidently discharged into his head while he was leaning on it. , D
651221	On the 14th inst., by Rev. Jos. G. Symmes, in the 1st church of Cranberry, John R. Mount to Miss Sarah E. Abrahams, daughter of John Abrahams, dec'd. , M
651221	On the 15th ult., by Rev. Jos. G. Symmes, in the 1st church of Cranberry, Abram Gulick to Miss Sarah S. Stults, daughter of Henry A. Stults. , M
651221	On the 29th ult., at the residence of Elias Dye, by Rev. Thos. D. Hoover, Simeon M. Stults and Miss Libby D. Cook, both of Cranberry, NJ. , M
651221	On the 23d ult., by Rev. Jos. G. Symmes, in the 1st church of Cranberry, Beakman Perrine to Miss Sarah E. Forman, daughter of the late Nelson L. Forman, dec'd. , M
651221	On the 29th ult., by Rev. Jos. G. Symmes, in the 1st church of Cranberry, Daniel P. Stillwell to Miss Rebecca E. Perrine, daughter of Henry Perrine, dec'd. , M
651221	On the 29th ult., by Rev. Jos. G. Symmes, in the 1st church of Cranberry, Wm. String to Miss Gertrude C. Long, daughter of Wm. Long. , M
651221	On the 2nd inst., at Imlaystown, by Rev. J. P. Connelly, Randall Brown of Windsor and Martha A. Haley of Clarksburg, NJ. , M
651228	At Hightstown, Dec 19th, by Rev. I. Butterfield, Chester Van Sickel of Flemington to Miss Mary J. Mount, of the former place. , M

Abstracts of the Deaths and Marriages in the *Hightstown Gazette*, 18 April 1861 - 28 December 1871

****

651228	At the parsonage, Dutch Neck, by Rev. A. L. Armstrong, on the 2d Nov, Charles Boyd to Miss Ussie Conover. , M
651228	At Windsor, Dec 20th, by Rev. I. Butterfield, J.D. Savidge of Hamilton Square to Miss Adaline Pullen, of Windsor. , M
651228	December 20th, by Rev. S. E. Post, George W. Brown of Pittstown, Salem County, to Miss Mary J. Vanhorn, of this borough. , M
651228	December 22nd, of consumption, Mrs. Anna Adelia Saley, wife of Melville Saley, of Windsor, in the 25th year of her age. , D
651228	Jesse Brown, an old citizen of Washington township, died at his residence in Windsor, on the 16th inst., at the advanced age of 88 years. , D
651228	Mrs. Emily Budd, died at Fresh Ponds, Dec 3d, 1865, in the 46 year of her age. Four years since she lost her daughter, Emily and two years and eight months since her husband died. She left a family of six children. , D
660104	On December 28th, of inflammation of the lungs, Wesley Cubberley, son of Enos Cubberley, aged 5 months. , D
660111	On the 3rd inst., by Rev. A. L. Armstrong, of Dutch Neck, Derrick Griggs of Harligen to Miss Cornelia, daughter of the late George Davison of West Windsor township. , M
660111	On the 4th inst., by Rev. A. L. Armstrong, of Dutch Neck, Sidney Griggs, of Princeton township to Miss Mary, daughter of Barzillai Grover of Cranberry Neck. , M
660111	On Tuesday, 2d inst., G. Vanderveer and H.C. Grover were gunning on W. R. Selover's farm near Rhode Hall, Middlesex county. They met a boy from the House of Refuge in NY, named Thomas Thompson, who worked for Mr. Selover. They parted and in a few minutes heard a gun shot. They found the boy, who was aged about 15 years, dead from a shot from the gun he had, which happened to be a gun belonging to Mr. Selover and had been taken from his house without his knowledge. , D

Abstracts of the Deaths and Marriages in the *Hightstown Gazette*, 18 April 1861 - 28 December 1871

****

660118	By Rev. Thos D. Hoover, assisted by Rev. A. L. Armstrong, at the parsonage at Cranberry, on the 11th inst., Henry M. Griggs and Miss Catherine Elizabeth McDonald, both of Middlesex county. , M
660118	By Rev. Thos D. Hoover, at the parsonage on the 21st of December, Firman Snedeker and Miss Sarah Ann Conover, both of Middlesex county. , M
660118	By Rev. Thos D. Hoover, at the residence of the bride's father, Enoch Pullen, Esq., Jacob Snedeker and Miss Carrie Pullen, on the 27th of December. , M
660118	By Rev. Thos D. Hoover, at the residence of the bride's father, H. Van Horn, John L. Peppler and Miss Sarah Van Horn, on the 3rd inst. , M
660118	By Rev. Thos D. Hoover, at the residence of the bride's father, Wm. S. Dey, Vincent C. Farr and Miss Josie S. Dey, on the 28th ult. , M
660118	In this borough on the 17th inst., by Rev. I. Butterfield, Alfred F. Hooper of Monroe, to Elizabeth Hutchinson of South Brunswick. , M
660118	Mrs. Mary Williams, 105 years, 9 months and 13 days, died near White House, Hunterdon county on the 28th ult. Her husband died 70 years ago. She had five children, two of whom died before her. , D
660125	At Allentown, January 20th, by Rev. Kneeland Ketchum, John Imlay to Mary E. Appleby, both of Cream Ridge. , M
660125	At Allentown, on the 15th inst., by Rev. Ketchum, Edwin Jimeson of Manchester to Miss Annie Norton of Allentown. , M
660125	At Hightstown, Jan 18th, by Rev. I. Butterfield, Jacob C. Pettie, of West Windsor to Miss Margaret N. Rogers, of the former place. , M
660201	In this borough on the 26th inst., Elizabeth N., wife of R. J. Ogborn, in the 52nd year of her age. , D
660201	On the 23d inst., at the residence of the bride's father, by Rev. A. L. Armstrong, of Dutch Neck, Selah G. Forman to Miss Jane, daughter of Isaac Rossell. , M

Abstracts of the Deaths and Marriages in the *Hightstown Gazette*, 18 April 1861 - 28 December 1871

****

660201	On the 31st ult., at the residence of the bride's father, in Washington township, by Rev. I. Butterfield, Voorhees Cubberley of Newtown, to Mercy A. H. Gordon. , M
660208	At Perrineville, January 30th, Mrs. Isabella Robbins, aged 78 years. , D
660208	By Rev. Thos. Hooper, on the 31st of January near Cranberry, Baird W. Applegate and Miss Jane E. Hunt, both of Monroe Township. , M
660208	Near the Plain Tavern, Feb 3rd, Jacob Perrine, aged 82 years. , D
660208	On January 18th, by Rev. W. M. Wells, at the bride's home, Jacob B. Lamberson of Keyport to Alice G. Davison, of Jamesburg. , M
660208	On January 21st., by Rev. W. M. Wells at the Jamesburg parsonage, Charles E. Davison of Jamesburg to Frances J. Hilton of Gravell Hill. , M
660208	On the 17th of January, by Rev. W. M. Wells, at the Jamesburg parsonage, Elijah Perrine to Margaret Ann Davison, both of Jamesburg. , M
660215	At the Parsonage, Dutch Neck, on the 7th inst., by the Rev. A. L. Armstrong, assisted by Rev. Thomas D. Hoover of Cranberry, William Hutchinson to Miss Hannah Kinsey, grand-daughter of Hugh Dunn. , M
660215	Feb 14th, by Rev. S. W. Hilliard, Albert T. Hughes, of Brooklyn, NY, to Miss Mary F. Johnston of Hightstown. , M
660215	In the Borough, on the 12th inst. of consumption, Court Voorhees, in the 44th year of his age. , D
660222	February 12th, near Hightstown, of consumption, Armenia Applegate, in the 19th year of her age. , D
660222	On February 15th, near Red Tavern, of diphtheria, George W. Ivins, in the 4th year of his age. , D
660222	On the 14th ult., by Rev. Jos. G. Symmes, John J. Stryker to Miss Kate E. Applegate, daughter of James Henry Applegate. , M

Abstracts of the Deaths and Marriages in the *Hightstown Gazette*, 18 April 1861 - 28 December 1871

****

660222	On the 17th ult., by Rev. Jos. G. Symmes, Wm. I. Ingraham to Miss E. Stults, daughter of Isaac Stults. , M
660222	On the 18th ult., by Rev. Jos. G. Symmes, John S. Mount to Miss E. Thomas, daughter of John Thomas. , M
660222	On the 1st ult., by Rev. Jos. G. Symmes, John G. Mount to Miss Emily A. Scelover, daughter of Abraham I. Scelover. , M
660222	On the 4th inst., by Rev. J. W. McDougall, George E. Pullen to Miss Lena A. Williams, all of Cranberry, NJ. , M
660222	On Tuesday, Milton Ives, Cornelius Ives, and John Applegate were hunting in a boat. Cornelius, about 18, attempted to draw his gun but the hammer caught on the boat seat and discharged and the load entered under his arm severing the brachial artery. He died about 4 hours later. He was the youngest son of John Ives of near Cranberry Station. Funeral tomorrow at Rev. Symmes' church, Cranberry [First Presbyterian Church, Cranbury, NJ]. , D
660301	Feb 15th, at his residence at New Sharon, Isaac H. Wilson, aged 97 years, lacking 23 days. , D
660301	On the 21st inst., by Rev. I. Butterfield, at the residence of the bride's father, Miss Emmaline Snedeker, of South Brunswick to A. E. Chamberlin of West Windsor. , M
660308	At the parsonage, Allentown, NJ, by Rev. Kneeland Ketcham, on February 28th, J.A. Tantum to Mrs. Sarah B. Hartman, all of Allentown. , M
660308	On the 1st inst., by Rev. J. G. Symmes, Isaac S. Bennett to Miss Mary A. McDowell, daughter of George T. McDowell, dec'd. , D
660308	On the 28th ult., by Rev. J. W. McDougall, Runey Conover and Miss Lizzie Applegate, both residing in Cranberry, NJ. , M
660329	In this borough, at the residence of William E. Brown, on the 27th inst., of typhoid fever, A. J. Emley, in the 41st year of his age. Remains to be taken to Jacobstown for interment. [In the 26th April issue a notice identifies him as "Andrew J. Emley".] , D

Abstracts of the Deaths and Marriages in the *Hightstown Gazette*, 18 April 1861 - 28 December 1871

****

660413	At the residence of the bride's father, Wednesday, April 4th, by Rev. J. Cochran, S.M. Hewlett, Esq, of Philadelphia to Miss Anna M. Peckham, eldest daughter of Rufus Peckham, Esq., of Oneida, NY. , M
660413	Near Milford, on the 29th ult., Widow Elizabeth Bodine, in the 90th year of her age. , D
660413	Near Red Tavern, on the 1st inst., of diphtheria, Emma, daughter of John Ivins, aged 4 years. , D
660510	Near Windsor, April 30th of disease of the heart, George Stile, aged 41 years. , D
660510	Rev. J. Kirkpatrick died at Ringoes, Hunterdon county on Wednesday last. He held the office at the Ringoes Presbyterian church for 59 years. , D
660517	At Milford on the 7th inst., Benj. O. Wilson, aged 65 years. , D
660517	At South Amboy, on the 15th inst., of typhoid fever, Mary V., wife of A.C. Emley, aged 27 years. , D
660517	In West Windsor township, on the 11th inst., Samuel Anderson, aged 70 years. , D
660517	On the 11th inst., near this place, Abijah J. Chamberlin, aged 69 years. , D
660524	In this borough on Thursday, the 10th inst., by Rev. I. Butterfield, Edward M. Bastow to Miss Sallie E. Gordon, daughter of Benjamin Gordon, all of Hightstown. , M
660607	On the 28th ult., by Rev. L. J. Rhoades, I. W. Carmichael, of New Sharon, Mercer Co, to Miss Lizzie M., daughter of Dr. L. Lane, of Tom's River, Ocean Co, NJ. , M
660621	Mr. W. W. Norcross, one of our oldest citizens, died Saturday after a sickness of several weeks. He formerly represented Burlington County in the Assembly, but has for many years been a resident of Trenton. He was in the 68th year of his age. , D
660705	At Cranberry, June 28th, by Rev. A. Gilmore, William Debow to Miss Elizabeth Decamp, both of Cranberry. , M

Abstracts of the Deaths and Marriages in the *Hightstown Gazette*, 18 April 1861 - 28 December 1871

****

660705	At the M. E. parsonage, Cranberry, July 1st, by Rev. A. Gilmore, Charles H. Silvers, of Hightstown to Miss Matilda Ann Perrine, of the first named place. , M
660705	Died - 1st Sgt. Geo. Thompson, Co H, 1st NY Cavalry, captured after re-enlisting and died at Andersonville Prison. , D
660705	Died - Albert Coolley, Co A, 6th NJV, died at Fredericksburg, May 14, 1864, of wounds received on the 11th at Spotsylvania, Va. He distinguished himself at Chancellorville. , D
660705	Died - Charles A. Coward, Co. G, 10th NJV, murdered in a rebel prison by a brutal guard at Lynchburg, Va., Oct 1, 1864. , D
660705	Died - Charles H. Lehming, Co A, Sixth NJV, died May 20, 1862, at Fort Monroe, from wound received at Williamsburg, which occurred on May 5, 1862. , D
660705	Died - Chas. M. Ford, Co F, 9th NJ, from exposure. Died at the residence of his mother in Hightstown, Aug 12, 1864, about one year after his discharge. , D
660705	Died - Frank Wilson, Co F, 11th NJV, killed at Chancellorville, on Sunday, May 3d, 1863. , D
660705	Died - George W. Jemison, Co. A, 6th NJ, captured at Spotsylvania Court House, May 13th or 14th. Died at Andersonville, Oct 24, 1864. , D
660705	Died - James Gorman, Co A, 6th NJV, mortally wounded May 13, 1864, and lived but a short time after receiving his injuries. , D
660705	Died - James Holman, Co. A, Sixth NJV, died March 20, 1862, at Camp Baker, MD, of typhoid fever. , D
660705	Died - James Reamer and Stephen Burns, Co A, 6th NJV, both killed June 1, 1862 at Fair Oaks. , D
660705	Died - John Gribens, Co I, 2nd NJ Cavalry, died at Natchez, Miss., in 1865. , D
660705	Died - John Williams, of Hightstown, enlisted in Co. E, 5th Reg. and transferred to Co. E, 7th Reg.. Died Aug. 19, 1864. , D

Abstracts of the Deaths and Marriages in the *Hightstown Gazette*, 18 April 1861 - 28 December 1871

****

660705	Died - Lt. Voorhees Dey, Co B, 1st NJ Cavalry, (promoted from Sgt. of Co. L, to 2nd Lt. of Co. B) killed May 28th, 1864, near Hawe's Store, Va. , D
660705	Died - Martin V. Robinson, Co H, 14th NJV, killed May 10th, 1864 at Spotsylvania Court House. , D
660705	Died - Patrick Shields, 3d Cavalry Reg., died at Newark Hospital, 1865 of chronic diarrhea. , D
660705	Died - Peter A. Jemison, James Carr, James M. Evernham, Co A, 6th Reg., were killed May 5, 1862 at Williamsburgh. , D
660705	Died - Richard Barker, Co. E, 2nd NJ Cavalry, died of typhoid fever at Natchez, Miss., Sept 15, 1865. A teacher by profession before enlisting. , D
660705	Died - Samuel F. Herbert, Co. A, 6th NJ, re-enlisted in Co. E and killed in front of Petersburg. , D
660705	Died - Theodore Anderson, Co E., 2nd Cavalry, died of starvation at Andersonville, Ga., Aug 28, 1864. , D
660705	Died - W.D. Rogers, Co. A, 6th Reg., taken prisoner Oct. 15, 1863, at McLean's Ford, and after one years confinement in Libby prison, Richmond, he died of starvation and the cruelty practiced on prisoners at that place. , D
660705	Died - Wm. H. Jemison (brother of Peter A. Jemison) Co. A, 6th NJ, killed in front of Petersburg, 1864, shortly after re-enlisting. He was at the battles of Williamsburg, Bull Run where he was captured, wounded at Williamsburg, and died in one of the , D
660705	Elwood R. Silvers, Co H., 14th NJV, killed at Winchester, Sept 19, 1864. , D
660705	In New York city, on Wednesday, June 27th, William S. McMorran, eldest son of John McMorran, Esq., of St, John, N.B.. He died of typhoid fever and was buried in Greenwood Cemetery. , D
660705	June 14th, by Rev. P. Cline, George Dennis of Ocean county to Miss Alice Malusbury of Hightstown. , M

Abstracts of the Deaths and Marriages in the *Hightstown Gazette*, 18 April 1861 - 28 December 1871

****

660705	List of East Windsor Township, NJ dead in Civil War -James Holman, Charles C. Lehming, Peter A. Jemison, James Carr, James M. Evernham, James Reamer, Stephen Burns, Frank Wilson, James Gorman, Albert Coolley, Martin V. Robinson, Lt. Voorhees Dey, John Williams, Theodore Anderson, Elwood R. Silvers, Charles A. Coward, W.D. Rogers, Wm. H. Jemison, Sam. F. Herbert, Richard Barker, Geo. H. Jemison, Patrick Shields, R. Coates Voorhees, Geo. Thompson, John Gribens., D
660705	On the 20th ult., at St. Peters Church, Freehold, by Rev. W.F. Nields, S. Mount Schenck, Esq. of Hightstown and Miss Mary Augusta, daughter of James Lloyd, Esq., of Freehold., M
660705	R. Coates Voorhees, Co. H, 1st NY Cavalry, killed in Upperville, Va., D
660719	Henry Silvers, of Cranberry, was drowned in the mill pond at that place, while bathing, on Sunday, 8th inst. He was a good swimmer and is supposed to have been taken with cramps., D
660719	Mathew McCullough was charged with the death of William Wilson, after the two got into a fight on the 4th and McCullough seized a plank and beat Wilson over the head. Wilson died on Saturday from the blow. Both Wilson and McCullough were residents of Washington Township. Wilson occupied a cabin in the "coalings" about 2 miles from Quaker Bridge and that is where the attack on Wilson took place., D
660719	On Sunday, the 8th inst., during a thunder storm, two of David Brower's young children were killed by lightning at their house on Metedeconk Neck, Ocean County. Their mother was injured but is recovering., D
660719	On the 2nd of May, by Rev. J. G. Symmes, Lt. Adrian Appleget, late of the 2nd, NJ Cavalry to Miss Ella M. Scudder, daughter of James Scudder., M
660719	Suddenly in this borough, on the 18th inst., Elizabeth S., wife of Rev. P. Cline, in the 40th year of her age. Funeral at the ME church and the remains will be taken to Glenwood Cemetery, Philadelphia, for interment. [The Reverend's first name is Philip., D
660726	Hugh McChesney, sexton of the Old Tennent Church, died at the residence of his son, William, near Manalapan Station on the 17th inst., in the 92nd year of his age.

Abstracts of the Deaths and Marriages in the *Hightstown Gazette*, 18 April 1861 - 28 December 1871

****

	He was baptized by Rev. William Tennent and was the oldest member of the church. , D
660726	On the 21st, in this borough, of Dysentery, Emma, daughter of Thos. L. Tibbs, in the 3d year of her age. , D
660802	George Raymond was murdered near Woodbury on Tuesday last. , D
660802	Hon. William V. Ward died at Long Branch of consumption on Sunday last. He was an active businessman and for a number of years in the Assembly. , D
660802	In this borough on the 27th ult, of dysentery, William W. Cole, son of Wm. Jones Cole, aged 1 year and 10 months. , D
660802	In this borough, on the 29th ult, Phebe, widow of the late Charles Johnston, aged 62 years. , D
660802	Near this borough on the 31st ult., Laura, infant child of William and Cornelia Allen, aged 7 months. , D
660802	Near this borough on Tuesday, 31st ult., Emeline, daughter of Isaac Goldy, Sr., in the 47th year of her age. , D
660802	On Thursday last, William Dawney, of Cedar Bridge, Ocean County, was thrown down and instantly killed. , D
660809	Laura, infant child of William and Cornelia Allen, died July 31st 1866. , D
660809	Peter I. Bergen, residing near this borough, died on Sunday last, resulting from injuries he received while reaping his fields due to an abscess that developed on the base of his spine. He was a young man. , D
660816	Aug 2nd, Rachel, daughter of Peter E. Wilson, aged 2 years and 6 months. , D
660816	Near this borough, on the 8th inst., Hezekiah Maple, aged 92 years. , D
660816	On Saturday, a young man named Hubb, stepped from the freight platform at Spotswood upon the train for South Amboy, but fell and his legs were run over by the train and he died later in the day. , D

Abstracts of the Deaths and Marriages in the *Hightstown Gazette*, 18 April 1861 - 28 December 1871

****

660823   Alfred Carmen, son of John D. Carman, born near Red Tavern, November 21, 1826. He was a carpenter and last built the house for his brother John. He enlisted in Co. H, 14th NJ, and was shot in the head, was buried on the field at Locust Grove, Nov. 27, 1863. , D

660823   Cornelius Booream, born June 28, 1815 in Somerset County and lived near Cranbury. He was in his 47th year when he enlisted in Co H, 14th NJ. He was killed at Locust Grove and was buried on the field. , D

660823   David Provost, son of Cornelius Provost, born in Cranbury, May 12, 1841, and joined Co H, 14th NJ and became Sergeant. He was wounded at Cold Harbor but killed at Monocacy, July 9, 1864. He was buried on the field. , D

660823   Elwood Silvers, son of Gilbert Silvers, born Aug 24, 1839, between Hightstown and Cranbury, but was living with his mother in Jamesburg, when he enlisted in Co H., 14th NJ. He was also killed at Locust Grove and was buried on the field. , D

660823   Franklin Burkly was born in Germany, lived near Jamesburg, when he entered Co H, 14th NJ. He died at Cold Harbor. , D

660823   George W. Cathcart was living near Dayton when he entered Co H, 14th NJ. He was killed at Cold Harbor. , D

660823   Henry A. Anderson, son of Joseph Anderson, born near Perrineville. He lived with Forman Perrine when he joined Co H, 14th NJ. He was drowned at Monacacy, Md., July 4, 1863. , D

660823   In this borough, on the 22nd inst., of scarlet fever, Henry Bowne, son of Mrs. Maria Bowne, aged 10 years. Funeral services at the M.E. church tomorrow, Friday. , D

660823   James B. Snedeker, son of Peter Snedeker, born near Jamesburg, entered Co H, 14th NJ. He was killed at Cold Harbor, June 3, 1864 and was buried on the field. , D

660823   James Little lived in the neighborhood of Jamesburg, when he entered Co H, 14th NJ. He died at Cold Harbor. , D

Abstracts of the Deaths and Marriages in the *Hightstown Gazette*, 18 April 1861 - 28 December 1871

****

660823   Jefferson H. Rogers was a member of Co H, 14th NJ, and was killed in the Wilderness, in May 1864 and was buried on the field. , D

660823   John Compton was born in Westchester County, New York, but came to live with an uncle in Englishtown, his father dying when he was young. He was a carpenter in Cranbury, when he enlisted in Co H, 14th NJ. He was wounded at Monocacy, July 9, 1864. He died a few days later and was buried in the hospital burial ground in Baltimore. He left a widow who soon followed him. , D

660823   John Henry Van Doren, son of Henry Van Doren, born near Cranbury, on 20th January 1828. He was a member of the Second Pres. church in Cranbury and was a mason by trade. He was killed at Cold Harbor of June 1st and buried on the field - Co H., 14th NJ. , D

660823   Joseph Jolly, son of Robert Jolly, born near Plainsboro and lived there when he enlisted in Co H, 14th NJ. He died at Locust Grove and was buried on the field. , D

660823   Marcus Aurelius Stults, son of Thomas Sorter Stults, born near Cranbury, 15 Sep 1840. He enlisted with his cousin, Capt Symmes H. Stults. He died at Cold Harbor, June 2d, 1864, and was buried on the field - Co H., 14th NJ. , D

660823   Patrick Kelly, born in Ireland and lived near Jamesburg, when he enlisted in Co H, 14th Reg. He was killed on the cars at Frederick City, April 1863. , D

660823   Rahselah M. Brown, a member of Co H., 14th NJ, died at Cedar Creek and was buried on the field. , D

660823   Symmes Henry Stults, son of Isaac S. Stults, born near Cranbury on 10 Oct, 1840. After early losing his mother, he was raised by his grandmother and aunt. He was an apprentice of Clark H. Silvers of Hightstown. Died July 9, 1864 and was buried on the field in Maryland - Co H, 14th NJ. , D

660823   Thomas F. Applegate, son of Forman Applegate, born near Cranbury, November 14, 1843. He lived with his father and was grown when he enlisted in Co H, 14th NJ. He fought in battles to Richmond, in Maryland, and others. He died at Cedar Creek on October 19, 1864. He was buried on the field. , D

Abstracts of the Deaths and Marriages in the *Hightstown Gazette*, 18 April 1861 - 28 December 1871

****

660823	Thomas Smith was living near Prospect Plains when he entered Co. H, 14th NJ. He died in the winter quarters at Brandy Station, February 1864. , D
660823	Thomas Van Hise was born near Dayton and entered Co. H, 14th NJ. He died at Locust Grove and was buried on the field. , D
660823	Van Wickle Griggs, son of Joachim Griggs, born Spotswood, but raised in Jamesburg, where he left his widowed mother when he enlisted in Co H, 14th NJ. He was captured at Monocacy but died in prison at Danville. , D
660823	William H. Sodon, born near Jamesburg, he entered Co H, 14th NJ. He died at Moncocacy and was buried there. , D
660830	A Miss V------, of Philadelphia, committed suicide in Rancocas Creek by drowning herself, on the 16th inst. She came from a wealthy family but was disowned and was buried in a pauper's grave. Her body was recovered near Bridgeboro where she was interred. , D
660830	Alfred Blake was born near Red Tavern in 1824. He joined Co K, 5th Reg.. He was wounded at Williamsburg, came home, but fever came on and he died May 30, 1862. He was buried at Hightstown. , D
660830	Alfred S. Perrine, the son of John H. Perrine, was born near Cranbury, Apr. 7, 1842. He joined the Co. M, 9th reg., in October 1861. He contracted typhoid fever and died on 10 April 1862 and was buried in Newburn, Va. with his comrades. , D
660830	At Compton's Corner, on the 25th inst., of dysentery, Georgietita, daughter of David N. Serviss. , D
660830	Austin W. Roberts, born in Pennsylvania but was raised in the family of Elbert S. Williamson, near Princeton Aqueduct. He joined Co G, 1st Reg. He was wounded and captured at Bull Run's second battle. He was paroled but then taken ill. He died at a hospital in Annapolis, where he died Dec 12, 1862 and there he was buried. , D
660830	Charles R. Stout, son of Joseph Stout, was born October 21, 1843. He enlisted in Co. G, 1st Reg., and was in several battles. He was wounded at James River, Va., June 27, 1862, died the next day and was buried on the field. , D

Abstracts of the Deaths and Marriages in the *Hightstown Gazette*, 18 April 1861 - 28 December 1871

****

660830 Edward S. Anderson, brother to Garrett Anderson, son of Matthias Anderson, was born January 25, 1845. He joined Co H, 1st NJ Cavalry. At White Oak Church, May 28, 1864, he was shot and killed instantly and was buried on the field. , D

660830 Garret Anderson, son of Matthias Anderson, born near Dayton, July 9, 1842. He joined Co H, 1st NJ Cavalry. He saw no action but died of disease contracted in camp in a field hospital near Alexandria, Va., March 28, 1862. He was buried in the field but died of disease contracted in camp in a field hospital near Alexandria, Va., March 28, 1862. He was buried in an unknown grave on the field. , D

660830 George W. Conover, son of Peter Conover, and older brother of Thomas J. Conover, was born near Cranbury. He was grown and married before the war began but enlisted in Co C, 1st Reg. He was in several actions and wounded. He was visited on the field by his father along the Rapidan in 1862-63, where he gave all of his personal belongings to his father. On May 4th, at Fredericksburg, he was wounded and died three hours later. He was buried on the field. , D

660830 Isaac Scudder Dey, the son of Isaac Scudder Dey, born near Plainsboro, and joined the 4th Reg. He was wounded, carried to Annapolis but died in 1864. He was buried in the Second Pres. church in Cranbury. , D

660830 Isaac V.D. Blackwell, son of Wm. H. Blackwell, born near Princeton, Jan. 19, 1840. He enlisted in Co F, 9th Reg. and was killed at Roanoke, Feb. 8, 1862. , D

660830 James M. Applegate, son of Andrew I. Applegate, born near Cranbury in 1829. He lived with his family near Red Bank and joined Co A, 38 Reg. He died in the area of James River, Va., in a hospital of consumption, on Nov. 17, 1864. He was brought home and buried in the 1st Presbyterian Church cemetery in Cranbury. , D

660830 James Rhoades, son of John Rhoades, was born in Monroe Township. He joined Co K, 5th NJ. He was killed at Chancellorsville, May 3rd, 1863. , D

660830 John E. Conover, son of Wm. V. Conover, born near Cranbury, Sept 30, 1844. He enlisted in Co B, 5th NJ. He was killed in the battle of Winchester, Aug 10th, 1864. , D

660830 John Henry Rue, son of Wm. Price Rue, born near Cranbury, Sept. 13, 1831. He was at Gettysburg and there wounded in the thigh on June 3d, 1863 but laid on the

Abstracts of the Deaths and Marriages in the *Hightstown Gazette*, 18 April 1861 - 28 December 1871

****

ground for two days and a night. He was then found but died on July 13th and was buried on the field. , D

660830   John T. McDowell, son of Thomas McDowell, born at Rhode Hall, Sept 26, 1836]. When grown he went to Stoutsburg, Mercer county and married and settled there. He joined Co H, 21st NJ. He was wounded in Fredericksburg, May 4th, carried back to Washington, where he died on May 11th, 1863. He was buried in an unknown grave at the hospital cemetery. , D

660830   Jonathan Holmdel, a well known resident of Monmouth county, died in his 75th year. He was a descendant of the noted Obadiah Holmes, who was 36 years the pastor of the Newport, R.I. Baptist Church, and who died in 1652. , D

660830   Jonathan Hunt, born in 1825, in what is today Mercer County, lived in the neighborhood of Prospect plains, where he left a family. He joined Co I, 1st NJ Cavalry and died on August 2, 1864 in a hospital near Petersburg, Va. , D

660830   Joseph M. McChesney, son of Thomas McChesney, born near Cranbury, Sept. 25, 1838. He early removed with his parents to Brooklyn, NY and worked for a jeweler, Platt & Co, in New York. He died in North Carolina, Aug. 14, 1865. He is buried in the Second Presbyterian Church in Cranbury and was a member of several units, one being the 9th NJV. , D

660830   Lewis D. Hughes, son of Joseph Hughes, born July 5, 1827, near Hamilton Square, but the family early removed to the neighborhood of Cranbury. He joined Co L, 1st NJ Cavalry and was in 26 battles and 16 skirmishes. He was wound ed at the Wilderness, June 6, 1864, died the same day and was there buried on the field. , D

660830   Perley F. Winchester, son of Asa F. Winchester, born at Dayton, November 24, 1841. He joined Co C, 1st NJ Reg. He was in several battles, captured and paroled. On May 4, 1863, in Fredericksburg, he was wounded and he was left on the field. This is the last his comrades heard of him. , D

660830   Price P. Blake, son of Thomas Blake, born January 29, 1839, at Dayton. He joined Co F, 1st Reg. At Spotsylvania, he was shot 18 times. His body was eventually recovered and buried on the field. , D

Abstracts of the Deaths and Marriages in the *Hightstown Gazette*, 18 April 1861 - 28 December 1871

****

660830   Robert F. Perrine, son of David Perrine, was born near Allentown. He joined Co H, 9th Reg., and was killed at Cold Harbor, June 3d, 1864. , D

660830   Sorter S. Stults, son of Peter Stults, born near Cranbury, Dec. 8, 1838. Early losing his father, he lived with his uncle, Thomas Sorter Snedeker. He joined Co. A, 9th Reg. In North Carolina, on May 16, 1864, in a battle at Drury's Bluff, he was listed as missing. It was said that he was sent to Andersonville and died there sometime in October 1864. , D

660830   Spafford Perrine, son of Henry Perrine, was born near Cranbury, March 3, 1840, and joined Co M, 9th Reg. He died of typhoid fever and died at Newport Barracks, Va., 23 May 1862 and was buried there. , D

660830   Thomas Dugan, born in Ireland, came to America about 1850, married in Cranbury and settled there. He joined Co M, 9th Reg. As the war was ending, he contracted typhoid fever. He went to Foster Hospital where he died April 30, 1865 and he was buried at Newbern. , D

660830   Thomas J. Conover, youngest brother of Geo. W. Conover, son of Peter Conover, joined Co C, 1st Reg. At the Battle of Spotsylvania, on May 12th, 1864, he was wounded in the bowels like his brother, and lived only a few hours. He was able to send a message home to his family by his pastor, Rev. James, in Cranbury. He was buried on the field. , D

660830   Ulsema Duncan, son of John S. Duncan, born near Plainsboro, Feb 11, 1836. Losing his father early, he had his home with his grandfather, Stephen Duncan, Sen. He was in business in St. Louis, returned, and then went into business in New York. He joined Co G, 71st Reg, NY Militia. He died after being shot in the head, July 21, 1861 and was buried on the field. , D

660830   William Clayton, son of David Clayton, Sr., born near Cranbury, Mar. 2, 1843. He joined Co M, 9th Reg., He contracted typhoid fever and was taken to Foster Hospital where he died 30 April 1865. He was buried at New Bern. , D

660830   William H. Silvers, son of Benjamin Silvers, born in Cranbury, Feb 2, 1846. He was in Co. A, 9th Reg., and died of typhoid fever on Aug. 1, 1864, in a field hospital before Petersburg, where is was buried. , D

Abstracts of the Deaths and Marriages in the *Hightstown Gazette*, 18 April 1861 - 28 December 1871

****

660830	William Morse, son of Garrett Morse, born near Prospect Plains, July 8, 1843, enlisted in Co K, 5 NJ when he was 19. He was at Yorktown and Williamsburg. He became very ill, was taken back to Yorktown and that was the last his friends saw him. , D
660830	William Vreeland, son of Cornelius Vreeland, born at Bergen Point, April 7, 1839. He lived there a the beginning of the war but then moved with his father-in-law, the late Wm. B. Reed, to Cranbury. He served time in NY regiments but also in Co G, 10th NJ Regiment. He was wounded at the Wilderness in 11 places and he died on May 24th. He was buried at Fredericksburg. , D
660830	Winchester T. Bennett was born in Burlington county but spent most of his life in Monroe township, and joined Co D, 1st Reg. He was in several battles but on June 25, 1862, he was killed at Gaines Mills, where he was buried on the field. , D
660906	Alfred H. Voorhees, elder brother of Robert Coates Voorhees, was born May 6, 1839 and lived in Cranbury when he joined Co H, 1st NY Cavalry. He took part in many battles including Gettysburg. But, in June 1864, he was captured below Petersburg, sent to Lynchburg and then on to Andersonville. He kept a record of his ordeal but the handwriting stopped for three days. Then another hand wrote that he had died on 12 August 1864. , D
660906	August 29th, near Wright's Saw Mill, of diphtheria, T. F. Johnson, son of Thomas Johnson, aged 2 years. , D
660906	Curtis Dunham, brother to Leonard W. Dunham, entered the 35th Regiment with his brother before he was 17. He was killed in the march on Atlanta in the battle of Big Shanty, June 15, 1864. , D
660906	George F. Labaw, son of Francis D. Labaw, born in Cranbury, Nov 21, 1843. He lived with his father and enlisted in Co B, 28th NJ, under Capt. H.S. Disbrow. He re-enlisted in the 9th Regiment and then in Co C, 3rd NJ Cavalry. The last letter from him was from Winchester, dated Aug. 4, 1864. He was captured, exchanged sick and sent to a hospital in Annapolis in March 1865, where he died on March 12th 1865. He was buried there. , D
660906	James C. Burt, son of Jacob O. Burt and grandson of Thomas Potts, was born near Manalapan, January 11, 1840. He was an apprentice carpenter in Cranbury and enlisted for 3 months, went to Elmira, NY and joined Co A, 141st NY Reg. After

Abstracts of the Deaths and Marriages in the *Hightstown Gazette*, 18 April 1861 - 28 December 1871

****

	many battles, he was wounded July 20, 1864 and died 6 days later. He was buried on the field in Georgia. A 1st Lt. commission reached camp after he was dead. , D
660906	John Thompson, son of Joseph Thompson, was born near Prospect Plains, Jan 15, 1842. He enlisted in Disbrow's Co B, 28th NJ, and was wounded at Fredericksburg, Dec 13, 1862. He was carried to a hospital in Washington, where he died Dec. 25th. His body was brought home and buried in Hightstown. , D
660906	Joseph Roth was born in Bavaria, Germany, in 1817 and came to this country in 1846, living in Cranbury for several years. He enlisted in Co H, 35th NJ, Sept 1863. He was taken ill, carried to a hospital in Mound City, Ill., where he died March 28, 1864 , D
660906	Leonard W. Dunham was born at Rhode Hall in 1844. Before he was 20, he enlisted in the 35th Regiment and was in Sherman's march on Atlanta. He was captured and died at Andersonville, Aug 26, 1864. He had a brother Curtis Dunham. , D
660906	Little Mary E. Donnell gone home. , D
660906	Peter M. Abrahams, son of Wm. Abrahams, of near Jamesburg. He was in New Orleans when the war began and was captured. He escaped and made his way home but on the way enlisted in Co K, 2nd Illinois Cavalry. He died of typhoid fever at Fort Massac on the Ohio River, Nov. 4, 1861. , D
660906	Richard Barker, son of Rev. E.M. Barker, born in Cumberland County, Feb. 23, 1829. He lived with his father at New Market and in Reading and Holmesburg, Pa. He was a teacher and came to Hightstown in 1852, teaching at Locust Corner and Cranbury. He entered the 2nd NJ Cavalry. In Sept., he was carried to Natchez, Miss. With typhoid fever, where he died on 14 September 1865. He was buried there and he left a widow and sons. , D
660906	Richard Cox, son of Wm. H. Cox, was born September 1835 and was raised in Cranbury. He then lived in Lawrenceville until his mother died and then moved to Worchester, Mass. and enlisted in a Mass. Regiment, and re-enlisted in 1864. He was killed at Shady Grove Church, June 3, 1864 and was buried on the field. , D
660906	Robert Coates Voorhees, son of Rev. Joseph Voorhees, was born at Allentown, NJ, Dec. 3, 1842. He was living near Hightstown and joined Lincoln Cavalry, NY,

Abstracts of the Deaths and Marriages in the *Hightstown Gazette*, 18 April 1861 - 28 December 1871

****

	in 1861. In a slight skirmish, in the Shenandoah Valley, he was killed. His body was recovered and sent home. He was buried in Allentown, May 6, 1863. He was brother to Alfred H. Voorhees. , D
660906	Sept 2nd, in this borough, of scarlet fever, R. Martin Petherbridge, son of Samuel and Nettie Caminade, aged 1 year and 14 days. , D
660906	Thomas Jolly, son of Robert Jolly, was born near Plainsboro, in 1834, where he married and settled. He was in Capt. Disbrow's Co B., 28th NJ, and was wounded in Fredericksburg, Dec 13, 1862. He died the next day and was buried on the field. , D
660906	William H. Craig, was born in Ireland in 1838, and his family came to this country in 1842 and to Cranbury in 1850, where he lived until moving to Ohio a short time before the war. He enlisted in the 84th Ohio and was captured in Chattanooga and at Chickamauga, Sept. 1863, he was wounded and left on the field. He was afterwards brought in and he died in a hospital Sept 28, 1863. , D
660906	Wm H. Pullen, son of Charles Pullen, was born near Cranbury, Mar. 31, 1836. He joined Co A, 6th NJ. He was never in action but was taken ill February and died at Camp Baker, March 5, 1862. His body was brought home and he was interred in the cemetery in Hightstown. , D
660906	Wm. Reed Herron, son of Thomas J. Herron, was born near Cranbury. He early lost his father and his mother moved to Cranbury. He joined Co B, 28th NJ. On Dec 13th, he was wounded at Fredericksburg and carried to a hospital in Washington. He was doing well but fever started and he died on Jan. 4, 1864. His body was brought home and interred in the cemetery of the 1st Presbyterian Church next to his parents. , D
660906	Wm. V.P. Davison, son of John D. Davison, was born near Dayton, Aug. 16, 1839. He lived with his widowed mother until joining Co B, 28th NJ. At Fredericksburg, he contracted typhoid fever, sent to Washington, where he died Feb. 17, 1863. His body was brought home and he was buried in Spotswood. , D
660913	By Rev. Thos. D. Hoover, in Cranberry, on the 5th of September, David Snedeker and Miss Caroline Spurling, both of Middlesex Co., M

Abstracts of the Deaths and Marriages in the *Hightstown Gazette*, 18 April 1861 - 28 December 1871

****

660913	A train accident one mile from Freehold on the Freehold & Jamesburg Railroad, on Wednesday, killed a young man, named S. O. Davison. , D
660913	At the parsonage, in Cranbury, on the 27th of May, by the Rev. Thos. D. Hoover, George Applegate and Miss Mary Louisa Sands, both of Middlesex County. , M
660913	In this borough, on the 12th inst., Mrs. Anna M. Page, wife of E. Cole Page. , D
660913	In this borough, Sept 13th, Mrs Phebe Hutchinson, widow of the late Rev. Sylvester Hutchinson, in the 85th year of her age. Funeral services at the ME Church. , D
660927	July 18th. by Rev. P. Cline, Charles H. Byard of Allentown to Miss Mary A. Terry, of Hightstown. , M
660927	Middlesex Lodge, No. 90. I.O.O.F., passed a resolution regarding the death of brother William R. Slover, who "died on the 16th of September after a brief illness". , D
661004	September 24th, by R. C. Robbins, Justice of the Peace, Hiram A. Grover and Miss Mary Pullen, both of Windsor. , M
661011	Commodore Robert Field Stockton died on Sunday at Princeton, NJ. Richard Stockton, his grandfather, was a signer of the Declaration of Independence and one of the victims of the British military prison during the Revolution. Robert was born in Princeton in 1795. [This is a long article regarding his career.] , D
661011	On September 12th, at the parsonage at Dutch Neck, by Rev. A. L. Armstrong, William Wyckoff of Rock Mills, of Somerset County to Miss Deborah, daughter of Richard Hutchi[n]son of West Windsor. , M
661011	Suddenly, by hemorrhage of the lungs, Thursday, the 4th inst., at the residence of Elias R. Conover, near Marlboro, Peter Wyckoff, of this borough, aged 28 years. , D
661018	At the Baptist Parsonage, Freehold, Oct 11th, by Rev. D.S. Parmelee, Mr. Clarence W. Sykes of Philadelphia, to Miss Angeline Errickson, of Freehold, NJ. , M

Abstracts of the Deaths and Marriages in the *Hightstown Gazette*, 18 April 1861 - 28 December 1871

****

661018	At the Baptist Parsonage, Freehold, Oct 11th, by Rev. D. S. Parmelee, T. Vaughn Crandall, M.D., of Newburgh, NY, to Miss Mary Adelaide Parmelee, eldest daughter of the officiating minister. , M
661018	Col. Charles J. Ihrie, State Librarian for several years, died at his residence in Trenton on Sunday last, in the 66th year of his age. , D
661025	At Westfield, Union county, Oct 10th, Lizzie A., wife of Dr. John B. Petherbridge, in the 39th year of her age. , D
661025	At Westfield, Union county, Sept 22nd, Ida Ruthetta, only daughter of Dr. J. B. and Lizzie Petherbridge, in the 15th year of her age. , D
661025	By Rev. Thos. D. Hoover, near Dayton, on the 17th inst., James P. Scranton of Petersburg, Michigan, and Miss Maggie A. Davison, of Middlesex Co. , D
661025	Died at Princeton, on Tuesday last, of typhoid fever, John A. Robinson, aged about 21 years. He was the son of John T. Robinson, Esq., of Princeton, the well known editor and printer. , D
661025	In Cranberry, by Rev. Thos. D. Hoover, on the 3rd inst., Thomas J. Perrine, of Hightstown to Miss Mary M. Vreeland, of Cranberry. , M
661025	In Freehold, on the 17th inst., of consumption, Miss Phebe, daughter of Joseph Murphy, Esq., aged 38 years. , D
661025	On the 18th inst., near Jamesburg, Mrs. Theodosia Paxton, in the 91st year of her age. , D
661025	September 23rd, by Rev. J.P. Connelly, Henry A Rogers and Miss Lydia G. Haley, both of Upper Freehold, Monmouth County. , M
661108	At Allentown, NJ, on Wednesday, Oct 31st, by Rev. K.P. Ketcham, Miller Coward of Windsor to Miss Mary Meyers, of Allentown. , M
661108	By Rev. S.S. Shriver, Monday, Oct. 29th. Vanzant Applegate and Miss Rebecca Ann Emmons. , M

Abstracts of the Deaths and Marriages in the *Hightstown Gazette*, 18 April 1861 - 28 December 1871

****

661108	In this borough, on the 29th ult., Marianna, daughter of Isaac Perrine, dec'd, aged 11 years, 4 months and 6 days. , D
661115	In this borough, on the 13th inst., of croup, Elsworth, son of Thomas Hall, aged 2 years and 6 months. Funeral services from the residence today. , D
661122	In this borough, on the 20th inst., of paralysis, Mrs. Elizabeth L. Ely, widow of the late Richard Ely, aged 54 years and 7 months. , D
661122	November 21st, by Rev. J. E. Alexander, Samuel M. Alexander to Miss Emma Norris, all of Hightstown. , M
661129	In this borough on the 27th inst., by Rev. F.A. Slater of Matawan, William H. Cottrell of Brownsville, Middlesex Co, to Miss Louisa C. Ely, daughter of the late Thos. Ely, of Hightstown. , M
661129	Margaret Kennedy, a servant in the family of Rev. C.D. Hartranft, died from injuries she received from a kerosene lamp which fell to the floor and broke setting her clothes on fire in New Brunswick. , D
661213	Attention is called to the advertisement of Farm of Israel B. Taylor, dec'd. , D
661213	In Hightstown, 26th ult., by Rev. H. Wescott, Abraham J. Clayton to Miss Abby A. Ely, both of Monmouth Co. , M
661213	In Hightstown, 28th ult., by Rev. H. Wescott, John I. Hulsart to Miss Hattie Hurley, both of Monmouth Co, NJ. , M
661213	Jesse Redman, one of the oldest citizens of Trenton died a few days ago. , D
661213	On the 28th ult., by Rev. Thos. D. Hoover, Aaron S. Vanderveer of Monmouth Co and Miss Mary, daughter of Isaac Brokaw, of Middlesex Co. , M
661220	At Keyport, Wednesday of last week, Mrs. William S. Murphy gave birth to three girls but one of them died. The others are healthy. , D
661220	Thomas Cole, an Englishman, Robert Camless of Cedarville, NJ, and Chas. Stackhouse, of Philadelphia, 3 of the crew of the schooner "Thomas Lumbard", were drowned in Delaware Bay of Tuesday. , D

Abstracts of the Deaths and Marriages in the *Hightstown Gazette*, 18 April 1861 - 28 December 1871

****

661227	At Bergen's Mills, Dec 18th, of whooping cough, Adalaide, infant daughter of George Cox, aged 2 years. , D
661227	At Milford, on the 30th ult., Mrs. Sarah Johnes, widow of the late Samuel Johnes, aged 78 years. , D
661227	At the house of the bride's uncle, Joseph S. Ely, Dec 25th, by Rev. J. E. Rue, Abijah C. Fisher of Mercer Co to Miss Lizzie Brown of Monmouth Co. , M
661227	On the farm of Peter Perrine, Joseph Rivers, colored, fought with the wife of another colored man named John Reddick. Reddick got a gun and shot Rivers through the heart. He was arrested for murder. , D
670103	At the residence of the bride's parents, near Dutch Neck, of Tuesday, January 1st, by Rev. A. L. Armstrong, William H. Harden to Miss Hannah Voorhees. , M
670103	The daughter of John Ely of Harlingen, (formerly a resident of this town), who was serious burned by her clothes catching fire from a kerosene lamp, died on Christmas day from her injuries, She was about 19 years old, and was expecting to be married soon , D
670103	The oldest Methodist in America, was John Schultz, aged 115 years, who resided in Pleasant Mills, Burlington County. He had been blind for many years but was vigorous until a short time before his death. , D
670103	Thomas Car, aged 14, who lived in New Brunswick, broke through the ice on Aken's Fish Pond, near Three-Mile-Run on Wednesday and drowned. , D
670103	Two lads, named Willie and James Bayard, were drowned while skating on a mill pond near Middletown Point after breaking through the ice. , D
670103	William Pew, an aged citizen of Mount Holly, died while sitting at the breakfast table on Monday. , D
670110	At Perth Amboy on the 1st inst., Lewis Compton, died upon his 84th birthday, in the same house where he was born in 1783. , D
670110	At the parsonage in Hamilton Square, January 1st, by Rev. Joseph Atwood, Joel M. Sprague to Miss Isabella Cranmer, both of Mercer county, NJ. , M

Abstracts of the Deaths and Marriages in the *Hightstown Gazette*, 18 April 1861 - 28 December 1871

****

670110	At the residence of the bride's father, Newtown, NJ, January 2nd, by Rev. Joseph Atwood, Enoch Cubberly to Miss Addie Wills, both of Mercer County. , M
670110	On the 12th ult., at the residence of the bride's father, near Sharon, by Rev. E. Waters, John W. Brown, of Page's Corner, to Miss Carrie M., daughter of Jacob Anderson of the above place. , M
670110	On the 1st inst., by Rev. Jos. Atwood, at the residence of the bride's father, Joseph E. Rue to Miss Clara, daughter of Allen Stewart, of Windsor, NJ. , M
670110	On the 24th ult., by Rev. Jos. Atwood, William S. Rue of Sharon to Miss Hannah, daughter of Azariah Reed of Windsor, NJ. , M
670110	On the 3rd inst., by Rev. Jos. Atwood, at the residence of the bride's father, in Windsor, Enoch K. Cole to Miss Hannah A., daughter of Israel Baldwin, of the above place. , M
670110	On the 6th inst., by Elias Riggs, Esq., David Anderson of Ocean to Miss Martha Cottrell of Monmouth county, NJ. , M
670117	At the parsonage on Wed., Jan 9th, by Rev. K.P. Ketcham, Charles W. Hunsinger to Miss Sallie L. Burtis, all of Allentown, NJ. , M
670117	By Rev. Thos. D. Hoover, on the 19th of December, Isaac B. Rowland to Miss Louisa A., daughter of Charles Groves, both of Middlesex County, NJ. , M
670117	By Rev. Thos. D. Hoover, on the 25th of December, James B. Mershon to Miss Margaret Ann, daughter of Baird Applegate. , M
670117	By Rev. Thos. D. Hoover, on the 27th of December, Charles Purdy to Miss Cornelia V., daughter of James Taylor. , M
670117	By Rev. Thos. D. Hoover, on the 9th of January, at the parsonage of the 2nd Pres. Church of Cranberry, NJ, Edward R. Davison and Hannah V. Wilson. , M
670117	December 25th, in Upper Freehold of croup, Sarah Stockton, daughter of Charles Stockton, aged 4 years. , D

Abstracts of the Deaths and Marriages in the *Hightstown Gazette*, 18 April 1861 - 28 December 1871

****

670117	December 2nd, by Rev. P. Cline, Charles F. Hunt of Perrineville to Miss Mary Ann Schuyler of Hightstown. , M
670117	Dr. John W. Woodhull, died at his residence in Princeton a few days since. He was about 60 years. We do not believe he was ever married. , D
670117	In New York, on Tues., Dec. 25th, at the residence of the bride's father, by Rev. Howard Crosby, James Walker of Cranbury to Lizzie Adams of New York City. , M
670117	January 12th, by Rev. P. Cline, David Kline of Bethelem, Hunterdon County to Miss Mary Jane Matthews of Jackson township, Ocean County. , M
670117	January 1st, by Rev. P. Cline, William H. Johnson to Miss Eliza Ann Gordon, both of Milford. , M
670117	Near Trenton, on Saturday, the 12th inst., of consumption, Lydia Ann, wife of James H. Everingham, and daughter of Peter Bodine, aged 33 years. , D
670117	On the 26th ult., by Rev. J. G. Symmes, Charles S. Farr to Miss Rachel A. Forman, daughter of Nelson L. Forman, dec'd. , M
670117	On the 26th ult., by Rev. J. G. Symmes, John Reid to Miss Catharine A. Stults, daughter of Isaac Stults. , M
670117	On the 3rd inst., by Rev. J. G. Symmes, William E. Bergen to Miss Cornelia Mount, daughter of V. W. Mount. , M
670124	Mrs. Abigail Potts of Recklesstown died on Tuesday at the age of 70 years. On the day after, her husband, aged 80 years died of paralysis of the heart. The latter was a shoemaker and was one of the oldest residents of Recklesstown. , D
670124	On Christmas morning, at the Jamesburg Parsonage, by Rev. W. M. Wells, Alfred Stonaker to Miss Lydia J. Soden. , M
670124	On January 9th, at the Jamesburg Parsonage, by Rev. W. M. Wells, Ezekiel Schenck to Miss Lydia J. Stonaker, all of Monroe. , M
670124	On Sunday, at the Pitman M.E. Parsonage, by Rev. R. Thorn, Andrew Terhune of Cranberry, NJ, to Mary Handley, of the same village. , M

Abstracts of the Deaths and Marriages in the *Hightstown Gazette*, 18 April 1861 - 28 December 1871

****

670131	At the residence of her son-in-law Wm. B. Johnson, in Manalapan, on Sunday, the 13th inst., Mrs. Marie Bilyeu, widow of the late Peter Bilyeu, Sr., of Hightstown, in the 84th year of her age. , D
670131	December 29th, at his residence on Cranbury Neck, Joseph Hunt, Sr., in the 89th year of his age. His descendants, at the time of his death, numbered over 100 viz: 14 children, 48 grand children, 41 great grand children. , D
670131	Estate of Elizabeth L. Ely, late of Mercer County, filed to bar creditors after a period of time. , D
670131	Near Englishtown, on the 11th inst., Sarah C., wife of Joseph Ker, aged 23 years, 7 months and 19 days. , D
670131	Near Milford, on the 21st inst., of croup, Elizabeth, daughter of George Embley, aged 17 months. , D
670131	Near Perrineville, on the 22nd inst., of typhoid fever, Mrs. Mary Anna Hunt, wife of Chas. F. Hunt, and daughter of Daniel Schuyler, of Hightstown. , D
670131	On Wednesday, January 23rd, by Rev. S.L. Finney, Charles H. Boud, of Farmingdale to Miss Jennie Jemison of Princeton, NJ. , M
670207	At Oconee, Ill., on Thursday, January 24th, 1867, at the residence of the bride's father, Oscar F. Rogers, Esq., by the Rev. A.V. Vandewater, Wesley T. Elliot to Miss Meloine Rogers, all of the above named place. , M
670207	By Rev. D.G. Mallery, Beverly, NJ, February 4th, Silas W. Clark of Philadelphia to Miss Jennie A. Bowne of Beverly. , M
670207	Died - At Oconee, Ill., January 28, 1867, Alfred Hutchinson, (formerly a resident of Hightstown), leaving a wife and three children -- He was buried with Masonic honors. , D
670207	Jan 23rd, by Rev. P. Cline, John W. Tindall to Miss Edith W. Rogers, both of East Windsor Township. , M
670207	Jan 31st, by Rev. P. Cline, George Emmons to Miss Sarah McManus, both of Hightstown. , M

Abstracts of the Deaths and Marriages in the *Hightstown Gazette*, 18 April 1861 - 28 December 1871

****

670221	By Rev. Thos. D. Hoover, at the parsonage, on the 13th inst., Theodore Veghte, of Griggstown, NJ to Mrs. Mary Ann Schwenger, daughter of Ralph Konover, Esq. of Middlesex county, NJ. , M
670221	In Cranberry, Feb. 15th, Peter Vandewater, aged 80 years. He was a member of the M.E. church of that village. , D
670221	In Cranberry, Feb. 13th, John C. Vanderveer, aged 77 years. He was the Ruling Elder in the 2nd Presbyterian church. , D
670221	On the 6th inst., by the Rev. Thos. D. Hoover, at the parsonage of the Second Presbyterian church, Cranberry, Henry C. Gravatt to Miss Mary Ann Amelia Mount, both of Monmouth county, NJ. , M
670228	At Hightstown, at the residence of Mr. David Dey, on Monday, the 25th inst., by Rev. S.S. Shriver, Charles Roth of Oregon and Miss Martha E. Conover, of Middlesex Co., NJ. , M
670228	Mrs. Coriell, wife of Dr. Wallace Coriell, of New Market, Middlesex Co., was murdered in her bed by the servant girl that she had just fired the day before. Mrs. Coriell was about 30 years old, had been married about three years, and had an infant child. , D
670307	At Milford, on the 19th ult., of consumption, Vincent Bodine, aged 61 years. , D
670307	At the parsonage in Hamilton Square, on the 3rd inst., by Rev. Jos. Atwood, Elwood B. Ayres to Miss Louisa Applegate, both of Hightstown, NJ. , M
670307	Miss Sarah Cooley, of West Milford, who was to have been married last week, died suddenly of inflammatory rheumatism, says the "Paterson Press". , D
670307	Mr. George G. Brown of Jersey City, who was to have been married Wednesday, dropped dead on Monday of heart disease. , D
670307	Near Hightstown, on the 27th ult, Mrs. Ann Chamberlin, wife of Abijah L. Chamberlin, in the 60th year of her age. , D
670307	On Sunday, 3rd inst., at the Baptist parsonage, Hamilton Square, by Rev. W. E. Watkinson, Samuel Flock to Miss Rebecca Tantum, both of Mercer county. , M

Abstracts of the Deaths and Marriages in the *Hightstown Gazette*, 18 April 1861 - 28 December 1871

****

670314	Feb 3rd, of typhus fever, at Carlisle, Pa., Col. John B. Petherbridge, MD, USA, in the 41st year of his age. , D
670314	Mr. Andrew McDowell died suddenly at his residence at Rhode Hall, Middlesex county, on Wednesday last. He was discovered by his wife having a night-mare, to which he was subject, and in a few minutes he was dead. , D
670321	In a Notice, it indicates that Margaret A. Konover and Richard B. Konover, are Administrators of the estate of Richard G. Konover, of Middlesex county, deceased. , D
670321	In this borough, on the 20th inst., Annie, daughter of William Warwick, aged 7 years, 6 months and 17 days. Funeral services at the M. E. Church tomorrow. , D
670321	Jacob Pittman, an old and well known citizen of Freehold, died at his residence on Monday last. , D
670328	Rev. Edward Page died suddenly at Keyport on Monday at the residence of Capt. Bishop. Rev. Page was about 80 years old. , D
670404	At Cranberry, NJ, on the 20th ult., by Rev. John Lowrey, Charles M. Dippolt, Jr, of Trenton to Miss Mary B., daughter of Benjamin Clark, Esq., of Cranberry. , M
670404	At Hightstown, by Rev. S. S. Shriver, Thursday, 28th ult., Melvin Saley and Elizabeth N. Zelwick, all of Windsor, NJ. , M
670404	By Rev. Thos. D. Hoover, on the 27th of March, John I. Wicoff and Mrs. Clarissa Griggs of Middlesex county. , M
670404	By Rev. Thos. D. Hoover, on the 28th of March, William Stults, Jr. to Miss Adelaide V., daughter of Enoch Pullen, Esq., of Prospect Plains, NJ. , M
670411	At the parsonage, April 4th, by Rev. A. L. Armstrong, Dutch Neck, at the residence of Mr. Nutt, in Cranberry, Peter Appleget of Princeton to Miss Ellen Davison, daughter of Sylvanus Davison of Monroe Township, Middlesex County, NJ. , M
670411	At the parsonage, January 1st, by Rev. A. L. Armstrong, Dutch Neck, James C. Reed of Lawrence Township to Miss Anna L. Knowles, daughter of Jacob Knowles, of West Windsor. , M

Abstracts of the Deaths and Marriages in the *Hightstown Gazette*, 18 April 1861 - 28 December 1871

****

670411	Near this borough, of dropsy, on the 1st inst., Mrs. Alice Ann Applegate, wife of Peter W. Applegate, in the 75th year of her age. , D
670411	Rev. James Wood, D.D. died at his residence in the borough on Sunday last. He was connected with the Van Rensselaer Institute as President. He was born 12 July 1799, near Sarasota Springs, NY. [See 18 April issue for long article on his life.] , D
670411	William Francis Faucett, formerly of this borough, was killed on Saturday, March 23d, while employed as a brakeman on the Illinois Central Railroad. His remains were interred in Oconee, Illinois. The deceased was in his 19th year and will be remembered as the little child deserted by his father and adopted into the Asher Hankinson family (formerly of Hightstown but now a resident of Oconee) and with him he lived until his death , D
670418	In Cranberry, April 6th, Harry Sanford, aged 21 years. , D
670418	March 27th, by Rev. P Cline, Charles W. Steele to Miss Mary H. McCoy, both of Bordentown, NJ. , M
670425	Charles Steward, aged about 70 years, and a resident of Allentown, committed suicide at that place on Friday by hanging himself. The deceased was of intemperate habits. , D
670425	Mr. G. F. Brown, formerly of New Brunswick, committed suicide at South Amboy on Sunday, the 14th. , D
670425	On the 7th inst., at the parsonage, by Rev. J. L. Kehoo, Francis W. Cole and Miss Lavinia Smith. , M
670502	In this borough, April 24th, of consumption, Catherine, wife of A. J. Ashton, in the 26th year of her age. , D
670502	Near Milford, April 17th, of consumption, Hannah, wife of Charles Roszell, in the 52d year of her age. , D
670502	Near Perrineville, April 19, of consumption, Susan Clark, aged 49 years. , D
670509	April 21st, by Rev. P. Cline, Henry Disbrow of Allentown to Elizabeth Terry of Hightstown. , M

Abstracts of the Deaths and Marriages in the *Hightstown Gazette*, 18 April 1861 - 28 December 1871

****

670509	Joseph Williams, convicted of the murder of John Reddick has been sentenced to be executed on July 5th. , D
670509	On Friday last, James Yeates, of Bakersville, Atlantic Co, killed his little grandson, aged 8, and then committed suicide by cutting his own throat. Yeates was originally from Pennsylvania, aged 63, the father of 11 children and the brother of a well-known merchant in Philadelphia. On Wednesday, he attacked another grandchild, Sally Yeates, with a hatchet and inflicted two serious head wounds. , D
670509	On Tuesday, Robert T. Hoy, of New York and Miss Mary R. Wall, eldest daughter of Hon. James W. Wall of Burlington, were married by Bishop Odenheiner, of St, Mary's Church in Burlington. , M
670516	John F. Deal of Philadelphia was killed on the Camden & Amboy Railroad, near Camden, on Thursday. , D
670516	Mr. Asher Hankinson, who removed from the borough to Oconee, Ill., a few years since, died at that place on the 6th inst., after a short illness of several weeks. [See 8 Aug issue for a long obit from an Illinois paper.] He was born near Flemington, NJ in 1803, joined the M.E. Church on the Trenton Circuit, moved to Allentown, then to Hightstown and then on to Oconee, Illinois, where he died 4 May 1867. He left a wife, son, daughter and six grandchildren.] , D
670516	Mr. Jeremiah Arose, aged 106 years and 14 days, was buried from the Methodist Church at Matawan, opposite Keyport, on Tuesday last. , D
670516	Near Magrillar Corner, 9th inst., of whooping cough, Emma, child of Thomas Chamberlin, aged 18 months. , D
670523	Died at the residence of his brother, Rev. E. J. Way, in Delaware City, Del., Joseph L. Way, in the 59th year of his age.. , D
670523	Hon. James Patterson of Monmouth county, died on Thursday, May 2nd, after a long illness. , D
670523	Near this borough, on the 17th inst., Willard, son of Samuel Ayres, aged 6 years. , D
670523	Rev. Thomas D. Hoover, pastor of the 2nd Presbyterian church of Cranberry died suddenly last night. [In the May 30th issue, it states that he died in Cincinnati on the

Abstracts of the Deaths and Marriages in the *Hightstown Gazette*, 18 April 1861 - 28 December 1871

****

22nd of May; and in 6 June issue, there is a long article of his life - He was born in Virginia and was buried in Cranbury in his own church graveyard.] , D

670523   The engineer of the Oil Cloth factory at Beverly, jumped from a train as it was nearing the station and was killed. , D

670523   Wm. Pearce, of Caldwell, one of the former Freeholders of this county, died on Friday. , D

670530   At Windsor, May 1st, by the Rev. T.C. Carman, John Emmons to Miss Frances J. McManus, both of Hightstown. , M

670530   At Windsor, on the 24th inst., Henry Snedeker, of consumption, in the 36th year of his age. , D

670530   On Monday last, Engineer Tobias Howell was killed along with the Fireman, in a train accident on the Delaware & Lackawana Railroad. Howell's remains were taken to Bordentown where his family, a wife and children, reside. , D

670530   On the 23d inst., by Rev. W. Margerum, at the residence of the bride's parents, John V. D. Beekman of New Brunswick to Miss E. Augustus, daughter of Robert W. Miller of Allentown, NJ. , M

670530   On the evening of the 22nd inst., at the residence of the bride's father, near Oconee, Ill., by the Rev. Wm. A. Wilbur, Charles M. Allen (formerly of Hightstown) to Miss Melvina Kirkbride, formerly of Bridgeton, NJ. , M

670613   August Fisher, a young man, living near Englishtown, committed suicide by hanging on Tuesday, the 4th inst. , D

670704   On the 12th inst., by Rev. Joseph G. Symmes, Charles A. Rogers of New York City to Miss Anna S. Disbrow, daughter of Capt. H.S. Disbrow, of Cranbury. , M

670711   Abraham Von Emburg committed suicide at Hohokus on Monday by hanging. During the late war, he was a Captain of Co B, 21st Regiment, NJV. He was about 35 years old. , D

670711   Joseph Williams, colored, was executed Friday last by hanging for the murder of John A. Reddick, also colored. The murder was committed on December 17th last year,

Abstracts of the Deaths and Marriages in the *Hightstown Gazette*, 18 April 1861 - 28 December 1871

****

near Tracey's Station on the Freehold and Jamesburg line, in Monroe Twp, Middlesex County. , D

670711 The body of Daniel O'Neil, a resident of Paterson, was found Friday at Pavonia Ferry, Jersey City, NJ. , D

670718 On Thursday past, John Bradley, aged 10, son of James Bradley, constable, living on Stone, near Proper Street, New Brunswick, was shot in a tree where he was eating cherries by one James McManus, son of the elderly couple owning the tree. The boy had asked and had obtained permission from McManus's elderly parents to pick cherries. The boy fell from the tree after being shot and landed on a shed roof where he was found dead. , D

670730 A child of Barzillai Pullen, formerly of this place, crept up to the track of the train, and had his arms cut off by the "dummy" train at the Junction in Princeton. The child died that same night. , D

670808 An investigation at the Almshouse in Paterson, NJ, showed that cruelty existed there and that those who died where all buried without an inquest. Some of those who died there were: Thomas Van Horn, Andrew Hamilton, Israel King, Isaac Billings, Mrs. Brophy and Mr. Fowler's gardener. , D

670808 Rev. R. G. Chase, formerly Rector of St Peters' Church in Freehold, was drowned at Ellsworth, Me., by the capsizing of a boat. His wife, daughter of J. R. Dobbins, of Mt. Holly, also drowned. Their daughter, aged 7, was not on the boat at the time of the disaster. , D

670815 At Long Branch, Monday, a run-away carriage caused three ladies to jump from it. One, Miss Mohn, died. , D

670815 Dr. George Taylor, USA, died at Galveston, Texas on the 5th inst. He was well known in Newark where he was in charge of Ward United States Hospital in that city. , D

670815 In Lambertville, 10th inst., by Rev. A.F. Hutchinson, G.B. Bergen of the Philadelphia Bar and Miss Isabella H. Winner, daughter of Rev. I. Winner, of the NJ Conference. , M

Abstracts of the Deaths and Marriages in the *Hightstown Gazette*, 18 April 1861 - 28 December 1871

****

670822	A conductor was killed Wednesday night on the Raritan and Delaware Bay Railroad after a bridge gave away and he was caught in the wreckage. , D
670829	Aug 26th - Troy. NY - A young man named Theodore Jones, assistant keeper of the prison in Hudson Co, NJ, was shot and killed in an altercation. Jones had been drinking. , D
670829	In this borough, on the 14th inst., William, son of John Holmes, aged 5 months. , D
670829	In this borough, on the 18th inst., John Albert, son of Daniel W. Perrine, aged 10 months. , D
670829	In this borough, on the 24th inst., Ada, daughter of Chas. H. Pembrook, aged 15 months. , D
670829	In this borough, on the 6th inst., Frank, youngest child of Rosteen Walton, aged 6 months. , D
670829	In this borough, on the 9th inst., Adaline, daughter of William Walton. , D
670905	David Gordon, Sr., died at Windsor of Friday, in the 84th year of his age , D
670912	In this borough, on the 8th inst., of consumption, Charles Ashton, in the 70th year of his age. , D
670912	Near this borough, on the 3d inst., of inflammation of the lungs, Andrew J., youngest child of Jacob H. Stults. , D
670919	In Cranberry, on the 9th inst., Stephen Duncan, aged 83 years. The last survivor of the old settlers of Cranberry Neck. , D
670926	In New York City, on Wednesday, Sept 18th, by Rev. William S. Mikels, Pastor of the 16th Street Baptist Church, Charles L. Robbins and Miss Josephine B. Walters, both of Trenton, NJ. , M
670926	James T. Jones of Hudson County was murdered by William J. Kirtley, who was sentenced to five years in prison after the jury found him guilty of 2nd degree manslaughter. , D

Abstracts of the Deaths and Marriages in the *Hightstown Gazette*, 18 April 1861 - 28 December 1871

****

671003	At Fort Morgan, Mobile Ala., of yellow fever, Joseph Ogborn, son of William Ogborn of this borough, in the 30th year of his age. Member of the 15th US Infantry. , D
671003	At Milford, Sept 19th, of inflammation of the lungs, Willie, son of Garret S. Tindall, aged 7 years. , D
671003	At the South Third St., M.E. Church, Williamsburg, NY, on Tuesday last, by Rev. J. B. Graw, Capt. James B. Morris, editor of the "Long Branch News", to Miss Jennie L. Brower of Williamsburg. , M
671003	On the 26th of September, by Rev. Joseph G. Symmes, Robert Redmond of Jamesburg to Miss Margaret Dey, daughter of Seth Dey of Cranbury. , M
671010	New Brunswick - Capt. Wm. Wilson and wife recently celebrated their 50th wedding anniversary; the marriage of their youngest daughter and baptism of 2 of their grandchildren all took place on the same day recently. Three sons are clergymen in the Reformed Dutch Church and one is a professor of music. , M
671017	At Milford, 9th inst., of consumption of the lungs, Rebecca, wife of Richard Waddy, in the 58th year of her age. , D
671017	Near Milford, 12th inst., Charles Roszell, of consumption, in the 59th year of his age. , D
671107	In this borough, September 7th, of consumption, George W. Coward, aged 39 years. Funeral services on Saturday morning. [See Nov 14th issue - He died of consumption and was aged 39 years, one month and twenty days and left a wife and family.] , D
671107	On the 17th ult., at the bride's father's, by Rev. Wm D. Hires, George A. Cole, of Windsor, in this county, to Adalaide E. Cook, of Upper Freehold. , M
671114	Jacob Vanarsdale, who murdered the boy, Baird, received his sentence on Tuesday. He is to be hanged on Thursday, Jan 9. [The Dec 5th issue stated that his sentence was commuted in the Somerset Co murder from death to life in prison on the grounds of doubting Van Arsdale's sanity.] , D
671114	Near Red Tavern, Oct. 29th, of paralysis, Mrs. Sarah Reed, of Trenton, in the 69th year of her age. , D

Abstracts of the Deaths and Marriages in the *Hightstown Gazette*, 18 April 1861 - 28 December 1871

****

671114	Near Red Tavern, Oct. 31st, Watson Hall, aged 60 years. , D
671114	Notice by the Administrator of the estate of Azariah Reed, deceased, Mercer County. , D
671128	Eight persons were killed in Bergen Hill, when contractors in the excavations for the new railway, were using glycerine and it blew-up. Eight were killed: John Hicks, blacksmith, leaves a wife and 7 children; Simmons, blacksmith; two Miller brothers, carpenters; Thomas Burns, foreman of blasting; and an unknown man from Jersey City; a boy named Ned Foster and another boy named Hugh. , D
671128	Notice by the Administrator regarding the estate of Charles R. Roszell, late of Mercer County. , D
671128	On the 21st inst., by Rev. A. L. Armstrong, of Dutch Neck, at the house of the bride's father, Furman Gordon to Miss Margaret Perrine, only daughter of William Perrine. , M
671205	In Colebrook, Ashtabula Co, Ohio, Sept. 25th, at the residence of her daughter, Mrs. Catharine Stults, wife of John Stults, aged 85 years. , D
671205	November 20th, by Rev. C. F. Worrell, at the house of the bride's father, David Gordon Clayton of Freehold Township to Miss Mary Ann Gravatt of Millstone. , M
671205	On the 3d of November by Rev. B. Phelps, at the residence of the bride's father, in Rome, Ashtabula Co, Ohio, Miss Susan A. Stults to O. F. Trent. , M
671212	A deaf and dumb man, named William Nutt, was killed while walking the Pemberton Railroad, a short distance from his home, yesterday. He was employed to work the road and had barely left his home, a short distance from this borough, when he was stuck by a train. , D
671212	On the 27th ult., at the residence of the bride's father, by Rev. A. L. Armstrong, of Dutch Neck, John Van Pelt of Jersey City to Miss Mary Grover, youngest daughter of Sylvanus Grover, of Cranberry Neck. , M
671212	On the 4th inst., by Rev. A. L. Armstrong, at the residence of the bride's uncle, Samuel L. Grove, near Plainsboro, Howell Stonaker to Miss Emily H. Grove, daughter of William Grove. , M

Abstracts of the Deaths and Marriages in the *Hightstown Gazette*, 18 April 1861 - 28 December 1871

****

671219	On Thursday, Dec 12, 1867, after a lingering illness, Isaac Pullen, in the 63rd year of his age. Funeral services from the Baptist Church with Rev. Cline of the ME church assisting. [In the 26 Dec issue, it states he married Jane Hulit, established his home near Hightstown in 1827 and he died December 13, 1867. Being the Universalist Church could hold the expected crowd, funeral services were held there as well as the Methodist Church. Also, the 27 Feb issue has an obit from "Gardner's Monthly".] , D
671219	The body of Charles Androulus was recovered on Friday and brought to Passaic. While walking home in a storm he fell into Berry's Creek and drowned. He had been pulled up but slipped and fell back in due to the cold. He was 23 years old. , D
671226	Dec 20th by Rev. P. Cline, Henry A. McKenna of South Amboy, to Christianna Bunting of Hightstown. , M
671226	In this borough, Dec 20th, after a long and lingering illness, John Bastow, aged 56 years. , D
671226	In this borough, Dec 23d, after a short illness, Hannah Conover, of Wyckoff's Mills, aged about 46 years. , D
671226	In this borough, on Christmas Day, by Rev. P. Cline, Henry Walters to Miss Ellen Schuyler, daughter of Daniel Schuyler. , M
671226	In this borough, on the 17th inst., Elizabeth Downs, aged 89 years and 10 months. , D
671226	Near this borough, on the 15th inst., Esther Ann, wife of George Laird, aged 30 years. , D
680102	Dec 25th, of convulsions, Lizzie, daughter of Randolph Chamberlin, aged 2 years and 9 months. , D
680109	At the M.E. parsonage, Hamilton Square, January 1st, by Rev. Joseph Atwood, Edward Parent to Miss Sittira Amanda Williams, both of Mercer County. , M
680109	At the parsonage, Hamilton Square, December 25th, by Rev. Robert S. Manning, Edward J. Earl to Miss Martha J., daughter of Wm. C. Lutes, all of Mercer Co. , M

Abstracts of the Deaths and Marriages in the *Hightstown Gazette*, 18 April 1861 - 28 December 1871

****

680109	At the residence of the bride's parents, on Christmas Eve, by Rev. W. E. Watkinson, John F. Robbins of West Windsor and Christia, daughter of J. B. Coleman, Esq, of Hamilton, Mercer Co. , M
680109	At the residence of the bride's parents, on December 11th, by Rev. W. E. Watkinson, Enoch Hutchinson and Eliza, daughter of J. Tindall Flock; all of Mercer County. , M
680109	December 1st, at the residence of the bride's mother in this borough, by Rev. L. Chase, Abijah Applegate and Miss Adelaide Ely, all of Hightstown. , M
680109	Jan 1st, at the house of the bride's father, Judson Hutchinson to Miss Eliza, daughter of James P. Allen of Washington township. , M
680109	January 1st by Rev. P. Cline, James McKenna of South Amboy to Miss Louisa Bunting of Hightstown. , M
680109	Near Hightstown, January 2nd, Mabel, daughter of Alfred Stephenson, aged six months. , D
680109	Sarah E. Spear, 3, daughter of Augustus Spear who keeps a beer saloon at Birnet street, New Brunswick, drank some laudanum and was found in the process. After being made to vomit, the child was put to bed thinking she was okay. She was found dead in bed in the morning. , D
680116	At Camden, on the 6th inst., William H., son of John H. Holman, aged five months and eleven days. , D
680116	In Princeton, Nov 17th, 1867, by Rev. John B. Hutchinson, Edwin Hill of Ewing, to Miss Angelina Hughes of Hamilton Square. , M
680116	In Princeton, Nov 20, 1867, by Rev. John B. Hutchinson, Frank A. Pullen of Hightstown to Miss Mary Davison of Princeton. , M
680116	In Princeton, on the 1st inst., by Rev. J. Macdonald, Joseph C. Sinclair of Hamilton Square, to Miss Hattie B. Nicholson of Princeton. , M
680123	On the 11th ult., by Rev. Joseph G. Symmes, William J. Stout to Miss Acsah E. Dey, daughter of Matthew R. Dey, deceased. , M

Abstracts of the Deaths and Marriages in the *Hightstown Gazette*, 18 April 1861 - 28 December 1871

****

680123	On the 15th inst., by Rev. Jos. G. Symmes, Charles Voorhees to Miss Lydia Ann Thomas, daughter of John J. Thomas. , M
680123	On the 15th inst., by Rev. Jos. G. Symmes, Levi C. Updyke to Miss Abbie S. Applegate, daughter of Anthony Applegate. , M
680123	On the 26th ult., by Rev. Jos. G. Symmes, John H. Covert to Miss Sarah J. Applegate, daughter of Abijah J. Applegate. , M
680123	On the 8th inst., by Rev. Jos. G. Symmes, Sydney Sickles to Miss Cornelia A. Voorhees, daughter of Peter Voorhees. , M
680130	Senator Providence Ludlam, of Cumberland County, NJ, died recently and it was announced on Monday last. , D
680206	In the borough at the house of W. J. Cole, by Rev. L. Chase, on the 29th ult., Edgar W. Read to Miss Elizabeth Jimison, both of Prospect Plains, NJ. , M
680206	In this borough, on the 4th inst., of apoplexy, Andrew M. Prevo, in the 61st year of his age. , D
680213	Mrs. Susan Johnes Clark of Lawrence Township died last week in the 74th year of her age on the estate were she was born and raised. In the early 18th century, Stephen Johnes, whose father emigrated from Wales and settled in Long Island and then came to NJ, married a daughter of Thomas Fitz Randolph, Esq. The estate still owned by the family, descended from father to son, and each was named Stephen Jones, but the line is ending with Mrs. Clark, the only child of the last Stephen Jones. , D
680213	On the 5th inst., by Rev G.P. Schetky, J. Madison Pullen of this place to Miss Willie M. Jobes of Pemberton, NJ. , M
680220	At the residence of the bride's father, near this borough, on the 5th inst., by Rev. J. Seger, Isaac H. Holmes to Mary E. Williamson, both of East Windsor. , M
680220	In this borough, on the 20th of February, Samuel Holcombe, after a lingering illness, aged 34 years and 9 months. Funeral services at the Methodist Church. He was a native of New Brunswick, NJ, but lived here for the past several years. He leaves a wife and four children. [27 Feb issue states that the funeral service was also the

Abstracts of the Deaths and Marriages in the *Hightstown Gazette*, 18 April 1861 - 28 December 1871

****

Episcopal burial service by Christ Church of Freehold and of New Brunswick. The 26 March issue, states that his wife's name was Ella W. Holcombe.] , D

680220   On the 12th inst., by the Rev. W.E. Watkinson, George Savage and Miss Sallie A. Nutt, both of Allentown. , M

680227   Feb 19th, by Rev. C. F. Worrell, at the home of the bride, Wm. F. Lott to Miss Euphemia M. Dey, daughter of the late Ruliff S. Dey, all of Monroe Township. , M

680227   In Alexander, NY, Dec 25th 1867, at the residence of the bride's father (Mr. C Strong), by Rev. D. Jackson, Walter H. Chase, of Springfield, OH to Miss Adele Strong. , M

680227   Obit from the "Gardner's Monthly" on Isaac Pullen of Hightstown - Isaac Pullen died on Dec 13th last, at the age of 62 years. This obit is more about his horticultural life and achievements but also describes his home in some detail regarding his plant arrangements around the estate. , D

680227   On the 23d inst., near Hightstown, Elmer P., son of Thomas Dey, aged 1 month. , D

680312   At Hightstown, on the 27th ult., of scarlet fever, Gertrude, daughter of Peter Wilson. , D

680312   Last week, the wife of David Lewis of near Sharpetown, Salem County, died from injuries suffered from an exploding kerosene lamp. , D:

680312   Miss Sarah Williams, age 20, residing with her mother at Florence Heights, near Bordentown, committed suicide on Friday by drinking strychnine. , D

680312   Near Milford, on the 29th ult., Samuel Butcher, aged 63 years and 6 mos. , D

680312   On the 4th inst., at the residence of the bride, near Windsor, by Rev. A. L. Armstrong, of Dutch Neck, Aaron Crawford of Windsor to Miss Sarah Vaughn. , M

680312   On the 9th ult., by Rev. W.B. Vanleer, near Prospect Plains, George McDowell to Miss Martha Black, all of Prospect Plains, Middlesex Co. , M

Abstracts of the Deaths and Marriages in the *Hightstown Gazette*, 18 April 1861 - 28 December 1871

****

680319	March 12th, by Rev. A. E. Ballard, assisted by Rev. J. S. Beisler, Rev. Philip Cline of New Jersey Conference to Miss Anna Sparks, daughter of Thomas Sparks, Esq., of Salem, NJ. , M
680319	On Saturday, Feb. 22d, James Ogden, at his residence near Pennington, NJ. , D
680319	On the 11th inst., by Rev. A. L. Armstrong, Dutch Neck, at the residence of the bride's father, George Ely Cubberley of Hamilton Township to Miss Mary Louisa, eldest daughter of Daniel Hawk, of West Windsor. , M
680319	On the 5th inst., by Rev. John B. Hutchinson, Henry W. Robbins of Windsor, NJ, to Miss Ann A. Bergen, of Stoney Brook, NJ. , M
680326	On Tuesday, March 24th, at the house of the bride's parents, by Rev. William Alvin Bartlett, George H. Griffin, of New York to Miss Lydia A.P. Hughes, daughter of Lambert R. Hughes, of Brooklyn. , M
680402	Administrator's Notice re: the estate of Elizabeth Tantum, late of Mercer county, dec'd. , D
680402	At the parsonage, in Dutch Neck, by the Rev. A. L. Armstrong, on the 28th of March, John V.D. Konover of Cranberry Neck to Miss Eliza S., second daughter of Judge Wm. G. Bergen, of the former place. , M
680402	March 30th, by Rev. B. S. Sharp, at Trenton, James G. Vaughn to Miss Sarah D. Chase, both of Hightstown. , M
680402	Near Cranberry, 1st inst., Mrs. Catharine Dye, widow of Lewis W. Dye, dec'd, in the 78th year of her age. Funeral from her late residence tomorrow (Friday). , D
680402	O. H. Fountain, a student at Pennington Seminary, died of paralysis of the heart on Friday last. , D
680402	On the 19th ult., in the Presbyterian Church of Manalapan, by Rev. J. L. Kehoo, Thomas E. Morris and Miss Nellie W. English. , M
680409	Near this borough, on the 27th ult., Elizabeth Van Marter, widow of the late Krion Van Marter, aged 74 years. , D

Abstracts of the Deaths and Marriages in the *Hightstown Gazette*, 18 April 1861 - 28 December 1871

****

680409   The little daughter of Thomas Ewart, who while playing on the Railroad Turntable had her leg and foot crushed, died of lockjaw on Friday evening. The incident was reported in the last issue of the paper. Near this borough on the 4th inst., from injuries received on the Railroad, Lydia, daughter of Thomas Ewart, aged nine years. , D

680416   In Pennington, March 22d, Sarah P., wife of Samuel T. Pullen, in the 32nd year of her age. , D

680423   At the Union Valley Church, on the 8th inst., by Rev. Watson, Elwood Van Dusen of Cranberry and Miss Maggie Brown, formerly of Long Branch, NJ. , M

680423   In this borough, on the 20th inst., of consumption, Elias Riggs, Esq., in the 57th year of his age. Funeral services were held at the Presbyterian Church. , D

680430   A small boy, about 6 years old, named Hoover, was drowned on Friday in Black's Creek, Bordentown, NJ. , D

680430   Anthony Johnson, who lately removed from this place to Manalapan, where he was in the employ of Mr. Danley, the miller, met with sudden death on Monday last, when he was thrown from the wagon he was driving and run over by the wheels. He served during the war in the 22nd Regiment, NJ Vols., and leaves a wife and 5 children. , D

680514   A little son of Isaac White at Atlanticville, aged about 2 ½ years was drowned in a spring house a few days ago. , D

680514   At New Sharon, on the 30th ult., of consumption, George A. Hall, aged about 45 years. , D

680521   Samuel Moore, of Hornerstown, was killed on the Pemberton Rail Road, one day last week. He was walking on the track and being quite deaf didn't hear the train. , D

680528   A man named Elisha Carr, of New Sharon, while intoxicated, was run over in Trenton by the Good Will Fire Engine on Monday last week and he died shortly thereafter. He was in the army during the war. , D

680528   Herbert W. Applegate died from the effects of the amputation of his arm at the shoulder, which was required after he accidently shot himself in the arm while attempting to crawl through a window in the barn with his loaded gun. The incident

Abstracts of the Deaths and Marriages in the *Hightstown Gazette*, 18 April 1861 - 28 December 1871

****

	occurred many weeks ago, with amputation put off until a week or so ago. However, he died on Friday. , D
680528	On the 14th inst., a son of Isaac Francis, who resides a short distance from Dayton, fell from a manure wagon, was run over, and died. He was 7 years of age. , D
680528	Richard Shippen, who died in Burlington on the 18th inst., was one of the pioneers in New Jersey railroading. , D
680528	The insurance company just paid Mrs. Rachel Ogden, widow of the late James Ogden, $1,000 death benefit. , D
680604	At Cranberry, on Wednesday, June 4th, by William A. Wakeley, Justice of the Peace, John Halpin to Francis L. Meyer, both of Imlaystown, NJ. , M
680604	By Morton McMichael, Mayor of Philadelphia, at his residence on Tuesday, 26th ult., William C. Norton of Hightstown to Mary Elizabeth Steward, of Yardville, NJ. , M
680604	By Morton McMichael, Mayor of Philadelphia, at his residence on Tuesday, 26th ult., Joseph S. Leland of Bucks Co, Pa, to Emily Tilton of Burlington Co, NJ. , M
680604	Capt. James Farrell was drowned at New Brunswick on Monday night after falling into the water intoxicated while trying to board his boat. , D
680604	May 31st, at the M.E. Church Parsonage, Allentown, by Rev. W. Margerum, Edward Savige and Miss Emma H. Pullen, all of Hightstown. , M
680604	On Saturday, May 16th, in the 21st year of his age, of Phthisis, John F. Fraser of Stillwater, Guysboro County, Nova Scotia. He was a student in the Hightstown Classical Institute and later an instructor in 1867-1868. , D
680618	In Hightstown, June 4th, by Rev. L. Chase, Charles Parker of Monroe to Miss Mary Eliza Winet, of Millstone township, Monmouth county. , M
680618	Mr. C.M. Norcross of Trenton died at Bellevue Hospital in New York yesterday after being found in the street in a state of paralysis. He was about 40 years old and leaves a wife and one child. , D

Abstracts of the Deaths and Marriages in the *Hightstown Gazette*, 18 April 1861 - 28 December 1871

****

680625	Edward Batten, a young married man of Mullica Hill, Burlington county, was thrown from his horse but his feet stayed in the stirrups and he broke his legs badly and they required amputation. However, he died. , D
680625	On the 16th inst., at the house of the bride's father, by Rev. J. W. Hassler, brother-in-law of the bride, Wm. H. Keeler of Hightstown, to Miss Annie Bilyeu, of Philadelphia. , M
680625	On Thursday, while a train was passing under the bridge near Monmouth Junction, brakeman George Waterman was standing on top of the train, and was killed when his head came in contact with the bridge. , D
680625	The wife of Patrick Hackett was killed near her residence between Newtown and Windsor on Thursday last, while trying to drive her cow from the train tracks. , D
680702	In this borough on the 20th ult., Mary A., daughter of Wm. Perrine, aged 2 years and 9 months. , D
680702	On the 22nd ult., of consumption, Julia, wife of Thomas M. Chamberlin, in the 24th year of her age. , D
680709	Rev. Winner, of the NJ Conference, died at Delanco, NJ on the 5th inst., in the 68th year of his age. [16 July issue states that he was Isaac Winner, born at beginning of this century, near Mount Holly, Burlington Co.] , D
680709	Wm. T. Hunt, an old resident of this place, died on the 3d inst., at the advanced age of 75 years, after an illness of several months. He was brother to Wilson G. and Thomas Hunt, of New York. His remains were deposited into the family burial plot in the old Baptist Church. , D
680723	A workman in the field of Cook S. Sonnard, above Pennington, died on Wednesday after being over-come by the heat. , D
680723	In Philadelphia, on the 18th inst., of cholera infantum, Israel Carl, son of Robert Purdy, aged 10 months. , D
680723	In this borough, on the 19th inst., Jos. I. Dey, aged 69 years. , D

Abstracts of the Deaths and Marriages in the *Hightstown Gazette*, 18 April 1861 - 28 December 1871

****

680723	In this borough, on the 20th inst., Lewis L., youngest child of D.B. Riggs, aged 4 months. , D
680723	Miss Mary Lamler[?] and Miss Annie Lavens were drowned in Atlantic City Thursday while bathing. , D
680723	On Monday, the body of the wife of Patrick Curley of Milford was found floating in the pond by the mill's flood gates. Both she and her husband had been "spreeing" it for some weeks and whiskey was at the bottom of it. She was at home in bed on Sunday after 12 o'clock but she was found missing early in the morning. During her wondering, she fell into the pond and drowned. Some years ago, she attempted suicide. She is survived by her husband and 4 children; one a year old. The jury rulled "death by accidental drowning". , D
680806	A son of John Wideman, aged 6 years, was drowned while bathing in the mill race at New Egypt, on Sunday the 12th inst. , D
680806	Henry Trough, a Mr. Vankirk and a son of Rev. Hosea Ballou, all of Philadelphia, were drowned at Atlantic City on Saturday last, while bathing. , D
680806	In this borough, July 29th of cholera infantum, Lizzie, daughter of Daniel W. Perrine, aged 6 months. , D
680806	Notice of thanks from the family of John W. Dey, who died. , D
680806	On the 2d inst., in this borough, of whooping cough, Margaret, daughter of Nelson Brown, aged 5 months. , D
680806	T. Salter Snedeker, Esq, of Middlesex County, died on Monday of cholera after a short illness, at his residence in Cranberry. He was a member of the Baptist Church of this borough. Years past, he was Assistant Assessor of the Internal Revenue for the 3rd Congressional District. , D
680813	Edwin A. Stevens, of Hoboken, died at Paris on Friday, 7th inst., in the 74th year of his age. His father was Col. John Stevens, who was a grandson of James Alexander on his mother's side. His 1st wife was a daughter of Rev. Picton of West Point and they had a daughter, Mrs. Garnet, who survives him. His 2nd wife was a daughter of Prof. Albert B. Dod of Princeton, who survives him. [Long article on his life.], D

Abstracts of the Deaths and Marriages in the *Hightstown Gazette*, 18 April 1861 - 28 December 1871

****

680813	Robert F. Kirby was struck by lightning while plowing a field near Imlaystown and was instantly killed. He was single and about 26 years old. [27 Aug issue states that Kirby was buried from the Baptist Church of Imlaystown. , D
680820	George Anderson of Haddonfield was drowned while bathing at Atlantic City. , D
680820	Miss Anna Mary Alexander, eldest daughter of Rev. J. E. Alexander, of the Hightstown Classical Institute, died after a short illness at the residence of her uncle, near Delanco, on the 17th inst. Her funeral took place at the Presbyterian Church in this borough. , D
680820	Mr. Reuben Griggs, an old resident of Cross Roads, Middlesex County, died at Cranberry on the 1st inst., aged 80 years. , D
680820	On Monday, at Bennett's Tavern, Shark River, NJ, William Woolley, intoxicated, got a shotgun and killed Hartson Fleming. He then cut his own throat. Fleming leaves a wife and several children. Woolley was having an affair with Mrs. Fleming. , D
680827	At Columbus on the 6th inst., by Rev. A. Mathews, Wm. H. Dennis to Miss Mary J. Holeman, all of Columbus. , M
680827	Mr. Garret Garrison, who resided near Dayton, was found dead in his bed by his wife. It appeared that suspicions arose and his body was exhumed and an autopsy was performed. No poison was found in his stomach. , D
680827	Ralph H. Shreve, Clerk of the US District Court, died Thursday in Trenton, after a short illness. , D
680903	On Monday, in New Egypt, at the house of Judge Jobes, Anna B., 16, and Hannah M., 12, daughters of Mr. Jobes, were instantly killed by a stroke of lightning while standing in a door looking outside. , D
680910	At Cranbury, August 19, Martha, wife of William Hutchi[n]son, aged 71 years. , D
680910	August 30th, at Perrineville, of dysentery Edward B. Perrine, son of Matthew Perrine, aged 17 months. , D
680910	Ebenezer Conover, of Freehold, was killed on the 31st ult, after falling 15 feet and breaking his neck. He leaves a wife and child. , D

Abstracts of the Deaths and Marriages in the *Hightstown Gazette*, 18 April 1861 - 28 December 1871

****

680910	George Gage, member of the Assembly from Morris County, died Saturday from typhoid fever. , D
680910	In South Amboy, August 17th, of consumption, John A. Applegate, in the 50th year of his age. , D
680910	On the 8th inst., in Newark, NJ, by Rev. R.R. Meredith, Rev. G. Hughes, of the M.E. Church at Hightstown, to Abby, daughter of John Van Name, of Newark. , M
680924	Annie E. Longstreet has been found guilty of manslaughter in Monmouth County for administering laudanum in May last, to George Griggs, infant son of Orsemus Griggs of Freehold township. Longstreet, aged 18, is from Kettle Creek, Ocean county. Her mother died when she was 3 months and she was brought up by her grandmother. Her father and grandmother were at the trial. , D
680924	At Perrineville, on the 21st inst., of consumption, Gertrude Bergen, aged 30 years. , D
680924	In this borough, on the 16th inst., Mary J., daughter of James Baremore, aged 3 months. , D
680924	John Rankin, about 20, son of Capt. James Rankin of Squan, was kicked by a horse in the bowels. He died on Saturday last. , D
680924	Near this borough, on the 19th inst., Mary, wife of David Allen, aged 80 years. , D
680924	On the 29th inst., by the Rev. A. L. Armstrong of Dutch Neck, George K. Laird, of Hightstown to Mrs. Ruth Blake, daughter of Daniel Davison of Dutch Neck. , M
680924	Wednesday, Sept 2d, by Rev. S.S. Shriver, Thomas D. Whipple, Esq., of Boston Mass., and Mary J. Vaughn, daughter of the late Lewis Vaughn of West Windsor. , M
681001	Mrs. Annie Stout, daughter of Francis Hopkinson, one of the signers of the Declaration of Independence, has just died at Bordentown at an advanced age. , D
681008	By Rev. L. Chase, Oct 2d, John O. Cooper of Bucks Co, and Miss Mary Scott of Hightstown. , M

Abstracts of the Deaths and Marriages in the *Hightstown Gazette*, 18 April 1861 - 28 December 1871

****

681015   In this borough, at the residence of the bride's father, on the 14th inst., by Rev. J. B. Turbin, John S. Silvers of Cranbury to Miss Annie P. Forman, daughter of R.R. Forman, Esqr, of Hightstown., M

681022   October 21st, by Rev. L. Chase, at the residence of the bride's parents, J. Henry Hyatt and Miss Jennie Anderson, all of Hightstown. , M

681029   Orpha Giberson died at this place on the 26th inst, in the 89th year of her age. She was called Aunt Orpha and had a hair-lip. She lived by herself and had her tombstone engraved and kept it at the foot of her bed. , D

681119   Public notices re: estate sales of Wm. J. Perrine, late of Millstone Township and Abijah J. Chamberlin, deceased. , D

681203   At Clarksburg, on 29th Nov of consumption of the bowels, Obadiah Eldridge, son of Aaron Eldridge, aged about 30 years. , D

681203   Emma Burns, a colored woman, threw herself on the tracks in front of a train and was killed near Camden by the Deep Cut. , D

681203   In this borough on the 8th ult., Catharine Eckley, aged 63 years. , D

681203   In this borough, on the 22nd ult., Ann, wife of Sidney Winant, aged 61 years. , D

681203   Near Danley's Mill, Nov 9th of dropsy, Samuel Mount, aged 60 years. , D

681225   At Milford, on Sunday, 20th inst., Amos Connett, in the 52d year of his age. , D

681225   December 16th, by Rev. A. L. Armstrong of Dutch Neck, at the residence of James Wyckoff, Isaac Hutchinson to Miss Eliza V. Wyckoff. , M

681225   On the 11th of November by Rev. A. L. Armstrong of Dutch Neck, at the residence of George Denison, William C. Cox to Miss Fannie C. Denison, both of West Windsor Township. , M

681230   At Crosswicks, Nov. 26th, by Rev. Levi Larew, Lawrence Reed of Recklesstown to Miss Henrietta Powell of Vincentown. , M

Abstracts of the Deaths and Marriages in the *Hightstown Gazette*, 18 April 1861 - 28 December 1871

****

681230	Dec 23rd, by Rev. W. Margerum, at the residence of the bride's parents, Abijah A. Anderson and Miss Theodosia Hulse, all of Mercer County. , M
681230	Dec 25th, at Windsor, by Rev. T. C. Carman, James Young to Miss Anna Oakerson, eldest daughter of David Oakerson, all of Windsor. , M
681230	July 24th, 1868, at Windsor, by Rev. T.C. Carman, Charles J. Taylor to Miss Sarah Ralph, both of Allentown. , M
681230	On Oct. 26th, by Rev. Levi Larew, George W. Wood to Miss Fanny Merrick, both of Crosswicks, NJ. , M
681230	On the 16th inst., at 13th St., Baptist Church, Washington City, by Rev. Howlet, John S. Smallset of Baltimore, to Miss Josephine A., daughter of John Myers of former city. , M
690107	By Rev. C.F. Worrell, December 16th, at the house of the bride's father, Abraham Britton to Miss Jane Gravatt, all of Millstone Township, Monmouth County. , M
690107	Jan. 7th, by Rev. Chase, Gilbert V. Ayres, of Hightstown, to Miss Cornelia W. Rodgers, of Dutch Neck, NJ. , M
690107	On the 22nd of December by Rev. A. L. Armstrong, of Dutch Neck, Ebenezer C. Updike to Miss Malvina A. Cox, both of West Windsor. , M
690107	On the 31st of December by Rev. A. L. Armstrong, of Dutch Neck, at the residence of the bride's father, William Hulse of East Windsor to Miss Maggie, daughter of Elias Updike of Windsor. , M
690107	On Thursday, 31st ult., at the residence of Walter Armstrong, Esq., Fair Hill, Cecil County, Maryland, by Rev. J. H. Johns, Dr. S.W. Morrison of Louisville, Pa, to Miss Sadie H. McDowell of former place. , M
690114	Near Cranbury, January 4th, after a long illness, Sarah Jane Ancelin, widow of the late Francis L. Ancelin, and daughter of Peter P. Stults, in the 41st year. , d
690114	William N. Woolley, convicted for the murder Hartshorne Fleming in August, was executed by hanging Thursday at Freehold. , D

Abstracts of the Deaths and Marriages in the *Hightstown Gazette*, 18 April 1861 - 28 December 1871

****

690121	On the 18th inst., at the Broad Street M.E. Parsonage, Burlington, NJ, by Rev. S.E. Post, David V. Fisk to Miss Achsah C. Gravatt, both of Hightstown. , M
690121	On the 18th inst., at the M.E. parsonage, Hightstown, Mrs. Eliza F. Westervelt, daughter of John Van Name of Newark, NJ. The remains are taken to Elizabeth for interment. , D
690121	Theodore Packer, about 18, a brakeman on a coal train, fell and was run over and killed a short distance from Jamesburg. , D
690128	On the 21st inst., at the residence of the bride's father, near Newtown, by Rev. T.C. Carmen, David Gordon of Windsor to Miss Emma Disbrow, daughter of Hendrickson Disbrow. , M
690128	On the 21st inst., by the Rev. A. L. Armstrong, Enoch Rue to Mrs. Elizabeth Shangle, all of Dutch Neck, NJ. , M
690204	At the residence of the bride's parents, January 27th, by Rev. Ketchum, John F. Mount of Hightstown to Miss Sarah Louisa, daughter of John L. Hendrickson of New Sharon. , M
690204	At the residence of the bride's father, Jan. 27th, by Rev. T.C. Carman, James C. Cole of Windsor to Miss Emma J. Coleman, daughter of Jesse Coleman of Hamilton Township. , M
690204	At Windsor, Jan. 31st, by Rev. T.C. Carman, John Zerwick of Windsor to Miss Mary Wilgus of Allentown. , M
690204	By Rev. Joseph G. Symmes, on 13th ult., James Farr to Miss Mary A. Stults, daughter of Thomas S. Stults. , M
690204	By Rev. Joseph G. Symmes, on 27th ult., Joseph W. Ervin to Miss Martha A. Dey, daughter of Ralph S. Dey. , M
690204	By Rev. Joseph G. Symmes, on Dec 23d, George Voorhees to Miss Mary E. Davis, daughter of John Davis. , M

Abstracts of the Deaths and Marriages in the *Hightstown Gazette*, 18 April 1861 - 28 December 1871

****

690204	By Rev. Joseph G. Symmes, on Dec 24th, George Applegate to Miss Anna V. Applegate, daughter of W. Applegate. , M
690204	By Rev. Joseph G. Symmes, on Dec 2d, Jacob Van Pelt to Mrs. Charlotte M. Lewis, daughter of Wm. I. Reid. , M
690204	By Rev. Joseph G. Symmes, on Nov. 15th, John M. Steele to Miss Alicia Thomas, daughter of Gilbert Thomas. , M
690204	By Rev. Joseph G. Symmes, on the 28th of October, Vincent Conover to Miss Louisa Applegate, daughter of Charles H. Applegate. , M
690204	Frederick Farr, who died at an advanced age, recently, near Cranbury, left a wife and 14 children. , D
690204	In this borough on the 4th inst., Kate, youngest daughter of Isaac H. Goldy. Funeral services on Saturday at the Presbyterian Church. , D
690204	In this borough, on the 29th ult., at the house of the bride's father, by Rev. L. Chase, Enoch Allen Rue to Miss Phebe Perrine, daughter of Alfred Perrine. , M
690211	In this borough on the 31st ult., Mrs. Theodosia Savige, in the 62nd year of her age. , D
690211	Isaac Dunn's body was found in the water pond Saturday near the Bridge Street bridge. [Probably Trenton.] , D
690211	On the 4th inst., at the residence of Isaac J. Snedeker, on Cranbury Neck, by Rev. A. L. Armstrong, J. Frank Murphy of New York City to Miss Laura Snedeker of Trenton, NJ. , M
690211	In Mercer County Court, William Smith. colored, was imprisoned for the death of a child of Anna Rice, colored. , D
690218	At Imlaystown, Dec 5th, by Rev. W.D. Hires, Jacob Sone to Miss Elizabeth McTowe, all of Monmouth County. , M
690218	By Rev. W.D. Hires, at the residence of the bride's father, Jan. 28th, John Chamberlain of Hightstown to Miss Ann M. Field, of Imlaystown. , M

Abstracts of the Deaths and Marriages in the *Hightstown Gazette*, 18 April 1861 - 28 December 1871

****

690218	In this borough, on the 12th inst., of inflammation of the brain, Robert Franklin, only son of John H. Silvers, aged 9 months and 7 days. , D
690218	In this borough, on the 31st ult., by Rev George Hughes, at the M.E. Parsonage, Garret N. Soden of Dutch Neck to Miss Maria L. Serviss of Cranbury. , M
690218	Joseph Smith of Trenton, was at Newtown on Saturday last, started walking on the track, while intoxicated, heading toward the home of a brother-in-law. While walking on the track, he was struck by a train and died. He was brought to this borough for interment. His wife was a widower who died a few years since., D
690225	At the Girard House, Philadelphia, on the 17th inst., by Rev. Thos. Stevens, Alexander Pullen of Lincoln, Del., to Miss Clara Russell, of Toms River, NJ. , M
690225	John McMurran, son of John McMurran of St Johns, N.B., and nephew of Joseph McMurran of this borough, died Dec. 28th, 1868. , D
690225	The oldest person in Mercer County and perhaps the state died on Thursday, a few miles from Trenton. He was Thomas Hewson, colored, died at the age of 112 or 116. He was born in Virginia and sold to service many times. The last being on the eastern , D
690225	Timothy McCarthy, living near Cooke's machine shop, Paterson, died on Sunday from rabies. He was bitten by his own dog. , D
690304	At South Amboy, on the 26th ult., James W. Forman, aged 35 years, son of R.R. Forman of Hightstown. , D
690304	In Mount Holly, March 1st, by Rev. James Waters, DeWayne Pullen to Miss Helen Norton, both of Hightstown, NJ. , M
690304	Mr. Eckerson died from rabies as reported by the "Paterson Guardian". , D
690304	On Monday, 22d of February, at the Parsonage, Sailor's Snug Harbor, Staten Island, by the groom's father, Rev. J. C. Jones, assisted by Rev. J. K. Campbell, W. P. Jones to Miss Kittie N. Pritchard, of South Norwalk, Conn. , M
690304	On the 24th ult., near this borough, of paralysis, Isaac Britton, aged 69 years. , D

Abstracts of the Deaths and Marriages in the *Hightstown Gazette*, 18 April 1861 - 28 December 1871

****

690304	On the 3rd of April, 1863, George W. Symonds, alias Charles Lewis, alias Davis, was hanged at Trenton for the murder of Mr. Romand. Before execution, he admitted to have been the murderer of Dr. Burdell. , D
690401	At the Methodist parsonage, Windsor, on the 14th inst., by Rev. T. C. Carman, Daniel Browers to Miss Jane Johnson, both of Bordentown. , M
690401	At the residence of the bride's father, on the 24th inst., by Rev. T. C. Carman, James B. Hall of Sharon to Miss Emma J. Stevenson, daughter of Alfred Stevenson of Hightstown. , M
690401	At the residence of the bride's father, on the 25th inst., by Rev. T. C. Carman, assisted by Rev. Turpin, George R. Field to Miss Ellie N. Hall, only daughter of James D. Hall of Sharon. , M
690401	Diphtheria has been prevalent in the village of Oakford, Ocean county, and one person, Thomas Lewis has lost three children to it in the past five days. , D
690401	In this borough, on the 22d ult., of consumption, Joseph Perrine, in the 37th year of his age. , D
690409	Near this borough, on the 8th inst., Arthur Howell. , D
690409	Near Windsor, on the 31st of March, Samuel Brown, in the 80th year of his age. , D
690415	April 7th, of diphtheria, Rebecca, daughter of George Embley, aged 8 years. , D
690415	At the Methodist Parsonage, 11th inst., by the Rev. G. Hughes, James M. Patterson of Jackson, Ocean County to Margaret Francis of Millstone, NJ. , M
690415	March 26th, by Rev. G. Hughes, Martin L. Ogborn to Mary E. Wainwright, both of Hightstown. , M
690429	April 21st, by Rev. S.S. Shriver, Edward Conover of Cranbury to Miss Mary Beekman of Hightstown. , M
690429	At the parsonage Dutch Neck, NJ, by Rev. A. L. Armstrong, on the 22nd inst., David Embley to Miss Alice Pierce, both of Cedar Creek, Ocean County. , M

Abstracts of the Deaths and Marriages in the *Hightstown Gazette*, 18 April 1861 - 28 December 1871

****

690506 At Smithville, on the 3d inst., William Lanning, aged 74 years. , D

690506 Garret S. Lewis, a native of Hightstown, and for a long time a resident of Chaseford, Ocean County, died suddenly at Cedar Creek, recently, aged 58 years. , D

690506 Near Red Tavern of consumption, on the 3d inst., Elenor, daughter of John I. Taylor, in the 22d year of her age. , D

690513 On the 4th inst., by Rev. Joseph G. Symmes, John W. Duncan to Miss Amanda Barricklo, all of Cranbury , M

690513 On the 5th inst., by Rev. J.L. Kehoo, at the residence of the bride's parents, Archibald F. Mount of Hightstown and Miss Almira Newton, of Monroe. , M

690520 In this borough, on the 6th inst., John S., son of Lawrence and Caroline Van Kirk, aged 7 months. , D

690520 Near Dutch Neck, on the 6th inst., of consumption, Katy Mount, daughter of the late Enoch Mount, aged 21 years. , D

690527 In Burlington, NJ, on the 14th inst., Elizabeth Applegate, widow of the late Andrew Applegate, in the 83d year of her age. , D

690527 In Cranbury, May 24th, Sarah E., wife of Wm. S. Appleget. , D

690527 In this borough, on the 19th inst., of consumption, Harriet L., wife of William H. Perrine, aged 29 years. , D

690527 Near Dayton, on the 23d inst., Margaret, widow of the late John S. Griggs, aged 77 years. , D

690527 On Friday, an engine on the Mt Holly & Burlington RR exploded and killed the following: John Sailer, conductor, leaves a wife residing in Mount Holly; Job Gaskill, engineer, leaves a wife and 3 or 4 children at Bordentown; Charles Platt, fireman, leaves a wife and 2 children at Plattsburg. , D

690527 Suddenly, in this borough, on the 19th inst., Susan Harris, aged 75 years. , D

Abstracts of the Deaths and Marriages in the *Hightstown Gazette*, 18 April 1861 - 28 December 1871

****

690527	The death of Wm. C. Howell, Esq. an old citizen of Trenton occurred last week. He had been Justice of the Peace, City Treasurer and Mayor of the city. , D
690610	An accident at Dunn's grist mill on Wednesday killed Mr. Dunn's eldest son, aged 13 years. He fell into the water-wheel and was crushed. , D
690610	On the 28th of April by Rev. E. D. Stultz, at the residence of the bride's parents, Ralph A. Dey to Miss Mary Lavinia Capner, all of South Amboy. , M
690610	The funeral of the late James Buckalew took place on the 2nd inst., at Jamesburg. His remains were interred in the cemetery established by himself at a short distance therefrom. , D
690610	The late pastor of the M.E. church of Englishtown, died in that village on Monday last in the 33rd year of his age. He was buried in the Freehold cemetery. , D
690617	Near Hightstown, on the 12th inst., of diphtheria, William, son of George Embley, aged 6 years. , D
690617	The wife of George McDowell, Esq, of Prospect Plains was killed last Wednesday while walking on the track in front of her residence. She was deaf, , D
690624	In this borough of scarlet fever, on the 19th inst., Mary Ellen, daughter of James Whitlock, aged 9 years. , D
690701	At Attlebon, Bucks Co, Pa., 22nd, Anna J. Morrell, daughter of Alfred Stevenson, in the 26th year of her age, of consumption. , D
690701	June 22nd, Bound Brook, James N., son of Nelson Silvers of Perrineville, aged 20 years. , D
690708	In Burlington, on the 4th inst., Joseph Cutter, formerly of Hightstown, aged 81 years and 5 months. The funeral services were held at the Baptist Church in this borough and the remains interred in Cedar Hill Cemetery. , D
690708	On the 26th June, at the parsonage in Dutch Neck, by Rev. A. L. Armstrong, Cornelius Grover to Miss Eliza J. Grove, daughter of Samuel S. Grove of South Brunswick. , M

Abstracts of the Deaths and Marriages in the *Hightstown Gazette*, 18 April 1861 - 28 December 1871

****

690722	In this borough, on the 16th inst., Mary Alice, daughter of Henry McKennis, aged 14 months. , D
690722	In this borough, on the 17th inst., of inflammation of the bowels, Orian, son of Charles Pembrook, aged 14 months. , D
690722	In this village on the 16th inst., William H., son of Melville Packer, aged 8 months. , D
690722	July 21, 1869, Hannah Margaret, wife of Garrett Hartman of Perrineville, NJ, aged 24 years, second daughter of John K. Whitmore, Esq., of New York city. , D
690722	Near this borough, on the 16th inst., Rachael, wife of John Harden, aged 23 years. , D
690729	In this borough, on the 20th inst., Clarence S., son of John Stonaker, aged 1 year. , D
690729	In this borough, on the 26th inst., of spinal affection, Charles F. Brown, aged 33 years and 7 months. , D
690729	On Wednesday, at Bordentown, two locomotives ran into each other, and a man named Reed (colored), who was employed on the train, was killed. , D
690819	At Cranbury, on the 14th inst., of hemorrhage of the lungs, Nelson Petty, aged 46 years. , D
690819	On the 11th inst., by Rev. C. F. Worrell, Daniel P. Hutchinson, son of the late Rev. S. Hutchinson, to Miss Jennie E. Fairbank, daughter of Dr. J. N. Fairbank, all of Hightstown. , M
690819	Stephen Pierce of Caldwell, NJ, was killed by lightning while walking on Sunday when a storm came up. He was the third member of his family killed by lightning. , D
690826	A German named Jacob Mock, in the employ of Peter H. Conover, a farmer residing near Freehold, attacked the Conover family earlier in the day. He was pacified but returned about 11 PM, swinging an ax and indicating he was going to kill them. As he attempted to attack the family, another employee handed Mr. Conover his shotgun.

Abstracts of the Deaths and Marriages in the *Hightstown Gazette*, 18 April 1861 - 28 December 1871

****

	Mock was shot in the chest and died. An inquest was held and Mr. Conover was exonerated by acting in self-defense. , D
690902	In this borough on the 31st ult., by Rev. J. E. Alexander, A. J. Ashton to Miss Mary Robbins, daughter of Charles Robbins, all of Hightstown. , M
690916	A lad named Decker, aged 10 years, was drowned in the Passaic River, by the Newark and New York Railroad bridge. Decker's father was the bridge tender. , D
690916	At the residence of the bride's parents, on the 1st inst., by Rev. F. Chandler, Thomas C. Swift to Miss Carrie A. Bowne, daughter of Mr. C. C. Bowne, all of Freehold. , M
690916	Joseph Archer, a resident of Fillmore, Monmouth County, died at Cream Ridge on Wednesday, after going down a well he had dug and was overcome by foul air. , D
690916	On Friday, 3d inst., John W. Kelley, passed away. He had had a short residence among us, his house having been in Philadelphia for many years past. He was baptized before his death by Rev. Hughes of the M.E. church. , D
.690916	On Saturday, Alfred Stevenson died from injuries he suffered after being thrown from a run-away wagon on Tuesday. His funeral service was held at the Presbyterian Church. , D
690923	Frederick Bransert fatally stabbed his two sons, John and Frederick, in the town of Union, NJ, on Thursday. , D
690923	George McCabe of Yardville, was thrown from his carriage on Sunday and was so badly injured that he died on Tuesday. , D
690923	In Wilmington, Del., September 8, by Rev. Alfred Cookman, R. Morrison Early to Miss Hattie W. Ogborn, both of Hightstown, NJ. , M
690923	On the 18th inst., at the residence of Capt. Gilbert Seaman, by Rev. J. B. Davis, Henry Rose to Miss Mary Ford, all of Hightstown. , M
690923	On Wed., Sept., 15th, at the residence of the bride's mother, by Rev. G. H. Vibbert, of Rockport, Mass., Wallace McGeorge, MD, and Miss Anna F., youngest daughter of the late Hon. Isaac Pullen, both of this borough. , M

Abstracts of the Deaths and Marriages in the *Hightstown Gazette*, 18 April 1861 - 28 December 1871

****

690930	In the woods, near Stoneybrook Bridge, a mile east of Pennington, the body of a stranger was found sitting against a tree. There were no marks or identification on the body and he was buried in that area. This all took place 40 years ago or more. And, now, the identity of the man, James Eberhart, is made known through the death bed confession found in the Manchester, England newspaper, called *The Examiner*. Eberhart came to this country and was looked up by a friend of his, Daniel Hulseman, who also came over from England. While walking through a wooded area near Pennington, NJ, Hulseman killed Eberhart for his money and sat his body up against a tree and left him there. , D
691007	A man, named William Nightengale, was shot and killed by James Serull, a negro, on the 6th in Phillipsburg, NJ. , D
691007	Near Perrineville, on the 25th ult., of croup, Charles A., son of Samuel Croshaw, aged 16 months. , D
691014	In this borough, on the 26th ult., of consumption, Elizabeth, wife of John R. Holmes, aged 30 years. , D
691021	Oct. 13th, by Rev. C.F. Worrell, in the Presbyterian Church at Squan Village, Charles W. Bergen, son of James M. Bergen, to Miss Zilpha E. Newbury, daughter of Tyler E. Newbury - all of Wall Township. , M
691028	Martin Voorhees, Esq., of Princeton was killed in an explosion of carbolic acid in Brooklyn on Monday. , D
691028	Sweeney, who was struck on the head with a wrench by James Murphy, about 2 weeks ago, died from his injuries on Wednesday in Trenton. , D
691104	In Bridgeville, Del., on Wednesday, Oct. 27th by Rev. J. F. Chaplain, F. Lemuel Buckelew, of Jamesburg, NJ, to Miss Ella S., daughter of the late Gov. Cannon. , M
691104	In this borough on the 29th ult., Lizzie Lawson, eldest daughter of Thomas L. Tibbs, in the 9th year of her age. , D
691104	In this borough, on the 23d ult., A. Lincoln, youngest son of Charles Keeler, aged 4 years and 3 months. , D

Abstracts of the Deaths and Marriages in the *Hightstown Gazette*, 18 April 1861 - 28 December 1871

****

691104	On Friday, while fishing, David Slocum, who resided along the coast and who was returning from Freehold, was drowned. , D
691104	On the 3d inst., by Rev. G. Hughes, at the Methodist Parsonage, Geo. L. Rogers of Hightstown to Miss Sarah R. Baker of Princeton. , M
691111	Dr. Isaac Pearson Coleman of Pemberton, died after an illness of 5 weeks on Thursday, the 4th inst., in the 65 year of his age. , D
691111	In South Amboy, Monday, an elderly lady, Margaret Greenleaf, set fire to her clothing and died on Tuesday from her injuries. She was a widow and leaves one daughter. , D
691118	In this borough, on the 6th inst., of consumption, Jane, daughter of John Hulse, aged 25 years. , D
691118	Maj. Augustus Perrine, late of the 10th NJ Vols., agent of C&A Railroad at Jamesburg, was killed Saturday after falling between a train. He was a son of the late Gen. John A. Perrine of Princeton, which is where he was buried. He leaves a family and widowed mother. , D
691118	Mr. J. Stults, residing in Old Bridge, was killed one day last week by a run-away team with which he was plowing. He was caught in the reins and dragged. , D
691118	Near Milford, on the 8th inst., of diphtheria, Emma, daughter of Schuyler Richardson, aged 4 years. , D
691125	A lad named Peter McBride of Chatham was killed Wednesday, when a train was thrown from the tracks after it left Chatham for New York , D
691125	Dr. William D. Newell, brother of ex-Gov. Newell, died at his residence at Imlaystown, Monmouth County on Monday last of consumption. , D
691125	Oct. 20th, by the Rev. A. L. Armstrong of Dutch Neck, David S. Johnson of Washington City to Miss Dorothea A. Combs of Dutch Neck. , M
691125	On the 17th inst., by Rev. A. L. Armstrong, at the residence of Liscomb T. Robins, of Dutch Neck, Nathan Allen of Neshanic to Miss Lydia R. Davison. , M

Abstracts of the Deaths and Marriages in the *Hightstown Gazette*, 18 April 1861 - 28 December 1871

****

691202	Conductor Parker, on a train of the NJ Railroad, stopped the train on Monday night to put off a constable of Harrison, NJ, named John Lane, who could not find his ticket and refused to pay. The train was stopped while on the Hackensack bridge and as Mr. Lane stepped off the train in the dark, he fell through an opening in the bridge and was drowned. His body was recovered the next day. , D
691202	Dr. John T. Woodhull of Freehold, died in Camden last week, in the 84th year of his age. He was the father of Judge G. T. Woodhull of the Supreme Court and Dr. A.W. Woodhull of Newark. A third son is a professor at Lincoln University. , D
691202	Leyman Allen, an old man, was found dead in bed, at Taylor Hotel in Jersey City on Thursday last. He was a retired merchant. , D
691202	On the 1st inst., by Rev. G. Hughes, Isaac R. Rogers to Mary S., daughter of Stout Ayres, of Hightstown. , M
691202	On the 25th Nov., by Rev. J. Jay, at Christ Church, Warwick, Orange Co, NY, J. Barclay Perrine of Windsor, Mercer County, NJ, to Miss Rosalie A. Stewart. , M
691202	Rev. D.V. McLean, Pastor of Presbyterian Church in Red Bank, NJ, died on Tuesday, Nov, 23d, in the 68th year of his age, having an afflicted companion and only son to mourn. , D
691202	The body of Dr. Frederick P. Auten, a dentist and chemist, in Trenton, was found in the canal at the State St. bridge, on Thursday last. He had been missing from his home since Tuesday. , D
691216	At the residence of the bride's father, near Windsor, on the 8th inst., by Rev. TC Carman, William E. H. House, of Lawrenceville, to Miss Hattie A., eldest daughter of Vanroom Rogers. , D
691223	In Cranbury, Dec. 15th, at the Methodist parsonage, by Rev. J.H. Stockton, Williard S. Cole to Miss Mary Elizabeth Walton, both of Cranbury. , M
691223	In Cranbury, Dec. 15th, at the residence of the bride's parents, by Rev. J. H. Stockton, in Cranbury, Cyrenius T. Clayton of Red Bank, Monmouth Co, to Kate R. Wilson of the former place. , M

Abstracts of the Deaths and Marriages in the *Hightstown Gazette*, 18 April 1861 - 28 December 1871

****

691223	In Cranbury, Nov. 3d, at the residence of the bride's father, by Rev. J. H. Stockton, John Silvers to Miss Edwina Cole, all of Cranbury, NJ. , M
691223	Notice by the Administrator of the estate of John Brown, late of Mercer county, deceased. , D
691230	Alexander McDonald, residing near Trenton, died from rabies on the 21st. , D
691230	At the Railroad Hotel, Dec. 25th, by the Rev. J.B. Davis, John Brown of Freehold to Mrs. Sallie Gamble of Hightstown. , M
691230	John Dickey, who was on Thursday convicted of murder, at Hackensack, NJ, committed suicide in his cell, the same evening, by hanging. This was thoughtful of John, as it saves the county some expense. , D
691230	On the 22d, at the residence of Mr. David N. Craig, near Cranbury, by Rev. C.F. Worrell, Wm. L. Stephenson, formerly of Hightstown, to Miss Kate R. Craig. , M
691230	On the 22d, by Rev. C.F. Worrell, Mr. Edward Lucas to Miss Carrie H., daughter of D. N. Craig, at the residence of her father, near Cranbury. , M
691230	On Wednesday, Dec 23d, by Rev. J. B. Davis, Benjamin Gordon to Miss Rebecca Mount, daughter of Abijah Mount, all of Hightstown. , M
700106	January 1st, at the residence of the bride's mother, Trenton, NJ, by Rev. R.V. Lawrence, James Mortimore Applegate of Raleigh, N.C., to Miss Anna J. Thomas, of the former place. , M
700106	John Layton and Joseph Page, who resided near Toms River, drowned in Barnegate Bay. Page leaves a wife and 5 small children and Layton leaves a wife and 3 children. , D
700106	On the 15th ult., by Rev. Joseph G. Symmes, Thomas Brocaw to Miss Rebecca Voorhees, daughter of Rev. Joseph Voorhees, deceased. , M
700106	On the 20th ult, by the Rev. H. Wescott, assisted by Rev. Doolittle and Rev. Mesick, J. Frank Westcott of Raritan to Miss Ella S. Carr, only daughter of A.H. Carr, Esq., of Somerville. , M

Abstracts of the Deaths and Marriages in the *Hightstown Gazette*, 18 April 1861 - 28 December 1871

****

700106	On the 22nd ult., by Rev. Joseph G. Symmes, in the 1st Presbyterian Church of Cranbury, Redford Gulick to Miss Kate Duncan, daughter of John Duncan. , M
700106	On the 9th ult., by Rev. Joseph G. Symmes, John Irwin to Miss Magie S. Applegate, daughter of Disbrow Applegate, deceased. , M
700106	On Wednesday, Dec. 28th, at the residence of the bride's parents, by Rev. Crum, Dr. A.S. Stoneberger, of Hightstown, NJ to Mrs. Mattie J. Bacon of Dayton, Ohio. [Her name may also be Hattie was reported in announcement in her hometown paper in Ohio. Her father was D. Altick, a well-known manufacturer in the area.] , M
700112	December 29th, at the residence of the bride's father, by Rev. W. E. Greenbank, Edwin C. Prickett of South Amboy to Miss Lizzie M., only daughter of Wm. Crammer, Esq, of Medford Township. , M
700113	At the residence of the bride's father, on the 5th inst., by Rev. J. C. Carman, William Rue, Jr, of Sharon to Miss Etta M., only daughter of Charles Danser of Windsor. , M
700113	In this borough, on the 1st inst., by J. S. Blavelt, Esq., John Jones to Miss Anna Daily, both of Freehold. , M
700120	Charles Bowker of Mount Holly died on Friday last while riding his horse looking for his cow. , D
700120	Edward Palmer, a citizen of Newton, NJ, died, and developed facts point to guilt of Mrs. Palmer and a man named Brown. He died on Tuesday of poison. , D
700120	Perth Amboy is excited about the elopement of James A. Gilman, father of 4 children, and a girl of 19. , M
700127	At Windsor on the 23rd inst., of consumption, Hannah Compton, aged 60 years. , D
700127	In this borough on the 23d inst., of consumption, Daniel D. Applegate in his 70th year. , D
700127	Mrs. Schwartz of Newark died on Friday from burns received by exploding kerosene. , D

Abstracts of the Deaths and Marriages in the *Hightstown Gazette*, 18 April 1861 - 28 December 1871

****

700127	Near Red Tavern, on the 23rd inst., Bertha, daughter of Abijah Dey, aged 4 months. , D
700127	On the 25th inst., at T. J. Pullen's, of consumption, Margaret Debow, aged 25 years. , D
700127	On Tuesday, a man named Eldsley, who was passing in a wagon, was killed by a train near Monmouth Junction. , D
700127	William J. Bottles, of Hamilton Square died last week from lockjaw. , D
700203	At Richardson's Hotel in this borough, on the 1st inst., of pneumonia and gastritis, Miller Elbertson, aged 35 years. , D
700203	In this place, Jan 27th, of paralysis, Kate H. Perrine, aged 33 years. , D
700203	In this place, Jan 27th, of scarlet fever, Elwood, son of John Silvers, aged 6 years. , D
700203	Lewis Hankinson of Tinton Falls, a farmer, aged 70, left his house to go to a neighbor's and was found dead on Monday on the bank of the Swimming River. , D
700203	On Saturday, a baker named Ocermiller, residing in Millburn, after getting off of a train, walked into a race-way and fractured his skull and was killed. , D
700203	On Saturday, near Bloomingdale, NJ, 12 miles north of Peterson, a man named "Blank" Nixon beat to death David Sisco during a quarrel. , D
700203	Suddenly, on the 1st inst., in this borough, of heart disease, Margaret Paxton, aged 66 years, a single woman. , D
700210	Jonathan D. White, a resident of Trenton, was working on a lathe when a piece of wood flew off the machine and ruptured his windpipe and he died. , D
700210	On the 19th ult, by Rev. Jos. G. Symmes, Job P. Thompson to Miss Amelia W. Stout, daughter of Charles Stout. , M
700210	On the 12th ult., by Rev. Jos. G. Symmes, Ables Edsall to Miss Charlotte J. Groves, daughter of Gideon Groves. , M

Abstracts of the Deaths and Marriages in the *Hightstown Gazette*, 18 April 1861 - 28 December 1871

****

700210	On the 25th ult, by Rev. Jos. G. Symmes, Aaron Snedeker to Miss Sarah M. Nealy, daughter of Thomas Nealy. , M
700210	On the 30th ult, by Rev. Jos. G. Symmes, Andrew Jackson Wikcoff to Miss Ada Voorhees, daughter of Abram Voorhees, dec'd. , M
700210	On the 30th ult, by Rev. Jos. G. Symmes, Thomas Shotwell to Miss Lizzie J. Stout, daughter of Charles Stout. , M
700224	At the residence of the bride's father, near Sharon, on the 20th inst., by the Rev. T.C. Carman, James McManus of Hightstown to Miss Anna Jane, daughter of Stewert Archibald. , M
700224	At the residence of the bride's parents, Shark River, on the 21st inst., by Rev. T. Taylor Heiss, DD, F. Van Nortwick to Miss Isbella White. , M
700224	Leonard Schwand, convicted of the murder of Conrad Stahl, in New Jersey, was sentenced to prison. , D
700303	Bernard Connelly, Jr., former resident of Freehold, died at Charity Hospital, NY, on the 7th, from hemorrhage of the lungs, in his 31st year. , D
700303	Jacob Betchner, builder, of Bridgeton, was so injured by being hit in the head with a board that he died. He was only 35 and a member of the Salem Methodist church. , D
700310	At Bergen's Mills, March 7th, of consumption, Taylor Dey, aged 28 years. , D
700310	At Manalapan, on the 28th ult., of spotted fever, Romaine, son of Romaine Hulit, dec'd, aged 6 years. , D
700310	At the Asylum near Trenton, on the 23rd ult., Alfred Lewis, son of John Lewis, of Perrineville, aged 23 years. , D
700310	In this borough, on the 25th ult., Gussie Moore, daughter of George R. Moore, aged 2 years and 6 months. , D

Abstracts of the Deaths and Marriages in the *Hightstown Gazette*, 18 April 1861 - 28 December 1871

700310	In this borough, on the 25th ult., of croup, Lizzie, daughter of Chalis Pullen, aged 2 years. , D
700310	John Cummings from South Amboy died in the Middlesex County jail of a burst blood-vessel. , D
700310	On the 25th ult, in this borough, of scarlet fever, George E., son of Thomas Coward, aged 8 years and 2 months. , D
700310	On the 2nd inst., in this borough, of scarlet fever, Joseph, son of Richard Baker, dec'd, aged 12 years 8 months. [Note: The headline reads "BARKER" while the name in the body reads "BAKER".] , D
700310	On Tuesday, near this borough, one of David Allen's children, a little girl about 5 years old, swallowed rat poison and died. , D
700310	Rev. John McClintock, Pres. of Drew Theological Seminary, died of typhoid fever at his residence in Madison, NJ on Friday at the age of 55. , D
700310	The death of Rev. Wm. T. Morrison of China, and son-in-law of Dr. S. E. Arms of Elizabeth, is announced. , D
700317	At Cranbury on the 15th inst., of bilious fever, Wille D., son of John B. Appelget, Esq., aged 20 years. , D
700317	At Hightstown, March 12th, by Rev. J. B. Davis, Nathan C. Sutton of Indiana to Miss Vashti B. Shinn of Mansfield, Burlington Co, NJ. , M
700317	In this borough, on the 16th inst., Annie E., daughter of R.R. Priest, aged 2 years and 10 months. Funeral services at the M.E. church tomorrow. , D
700317	On Saturday, the wife of Patrick Geary committed suicide by slicing her abdomen with a razor so that her intestines came out. , D
700317	Rev. J. C. Pratt, Methodist, died on Wednesday at his residence in Jersey City, in his 90th year. , D
700324	At Windsor on the 19th inst., by Rev. T.C. Carman, Edward G. Hamilton, of Cranbury Neck to Miss Mary L., daughter of James Emmons of Windsor. , M

Abstracts of the Deaths and Marriages in the *Hightstown Gazette*, 18 April 1861 - 28 December 1871

****

700331	At Milford, on the 26th, of scarlet fever, Garrett, son of John Maple, aged 5 years. , D
700331	At Oconee, Ill., on the 20th inst., Melvina F., wife of Charles M. Allen, aged 23 years. , D
700331	Barnegat - March 21 - Capt. James Anderson and Mr. Cabrin, of Waretown, were drowned. On Sat., Wm. H. Cranmer of Manahawkin was drowned 2 miles below Tom's River and was Mr. Martin. Benjamin Hazleton lost a son. , D
700331	March 23d, Charles Irvin, son of Edward Irvin, aged 10 months. , D
700331	March 24th, by Rev. J. S. Van Dyke, at the residence of Richard Dey, Prospect Plains, John M. Lucas of Manalapan, to Miss Sarah Ann Dey of Prospect Plains, NJ. , M
700331	March 25th, near Cranbury, Anna E., daughter of Thomas Coward, aged 5 years. , D
700331	March 3d, by Rev. J. S. Van Dyke, at the residence of the bride's father, Plainsboro, NJ, Sylvanus Grover, Jr. to Miss Kate Cox. , M
700331	Mr. D.A. Holmes of Tinton Falls, Monmouth County, died on Friday. , D
700407	At the Asylum, near Trenton, on the 4th inst., David L. Conover, aged 63 years. , D
700407	In this borough, April 6th, Bertie Dawes, daughter of Aaron and Josephine Dawes, in the 4th year of her age. Funeral services at the Presbyterian Church. , D
700407	In Uniontown, Woodbridge Twp, Middlesex County, NJ, Edward Baldwin, the father, and Wm. Baldwin, his son, both living in New York, married Mrs. Ann Randolph, the mother, and Miss Mary Randolph, the daughter, on Thursday, March 24, 1870. , M
700407	Jan. 16th, by Rev. T.C. Carman, James M. Hill to Miss Sarah Forman, both of Edinburg. , M
700407	Michael Hay at Jersey City committed suicide by drinking nitric acid. , D

Abstracts of the Deaths and Marriages in the *Hightstown Gazette*, 18 April 1861 - 28 December 1871

****

700407	On the 23d inst., in the town of Parsipppany, Mr. and Mrs. Stephen Righter, died within a day of each other, aged 84 and 70, respectively, after 50 years of marriage. , D
700407	Robert Ayres died last week at his residence near this borough at an advanced age. He was the father of 24, the grandfather of 63, and the great-grandfather of 28. , D
700414	Mary Jones, an apprentice girl, living with Mr. T.S. Mount, near Wyckoff's Mills, came to her death on Friday last. , D
700421	In this borough, April 14th, Nettie, daughter of Aaron and Josephine Dawes, aged 10 years and 2 months. , D
700421	Mr. Alex Newbold, a resident of Wrightstown, committed suicide on Sunday last by hanging himself in an outbuilding. , D
700421	Taro Kusacabe of Achizen, Japan, a student at Rutgers College, died Wednesday of consumption, in the 22d year of his age. , D
700428	A Mrs. Genreux died from poisoning in Jersey City of Friday after drinking gin in which mandrake root had been soaked. , D
700428	A young lady of 17, a Miss Perrine, died a few days ago. She was the daughter of the man crushed by freight cars in Jamesburg last year. , D
700428	At Cranbury, on the 24th inst., Mrs. Elizabeth Lanning, in the 83rd year of her age. , D
700428	On Wednesday last, Mrs. Halloran was found dead at her residence at Hickory Hill, near Boonton, NJ, and it is believed to be murder by her husband, Thomas Halloran. He was from County Clare, Ireland and is about 45 years old. He was a miner previously. , D
700428	Richard R. Ely, of near Jerseyville, Ill., died on the 22nd of January. He removed to that place from Monmouth Co, NJ, in 1848. , D
700428	Sally Jelf, born in Elizabeth, NJ, March 27, 1766, died at 104 years old. Her father was an Englishman engaged in the mercantile business. , D

Abstracts of the Deaths and Marriages in the *Hightstown Gazette*, 18 April 1861 - 28 December 1871

****

700505	At Toms River, on the 28th ult, of consumption, Rachel W. Carmichael, aged 64 years. , D
700505	In this borough on the 28th ult., Elizabeth T. Brown, wife of Taylor Brown in the 47th year of her age. , D
700512	Miss Emily Pancoast, a descendant of the original settlers of Bordentown, died in that city a few days ago. , D
700512	Nelson Beers, a boy of 14, was thrown from a wagon in Freehold and was killed a few days ago. , D
700512	On Monday last, Mrs. Cornelius Irvin of near Englishtown, had an apparent stroke. She died on Tuesday. , D
700512	On Sunday, Daniel Lake, of Philadelphia, died at Trenton, NJ, after becoming intoxicated and falling down he cut is arm severing an artery. He died later that Saturday night. , D
700512	Stephen Herbert, of Old Bridge, was buried with Masonic honors from that place on Thursday last. , D
700512	Thomas Connell, a laborer on the C&A Rail Road, at South Amboy, fell under a gravel car and was killed. , D
700519	Captain N.D. Thompson, formerly commander of the steamboat "Richard Stockton" died on Monday at Bordentown. , D
700519	George W. Pillow of Springdale, Pa., a member of the Junior class of Princeton died on Sunday of heart disease. , D
700519	On Monday, Enoch R. Borden, Esq, died at his residence in Trenton. He was 49 year old and was never married. He was editor of the "State Gazette". , D
700526	Daniel H. Campbell, a colored man, died at Burlington, a few days since, aged 102 years. , D
700526	Isaac Dobbins, a bachelor, of near Mount Holly, was found dead in his ed on Friday. , D

Abstracts of the Deaths and Marriages in the *Hightstown Gazette*, 18 April 1861 - 28 December 1871

****

700526	John B. Adams of Pleasantville, a young man of 21 years, was killed when caught between two cars at Winslow on Saturday. , D
700526	On Friday, a farmer named Merryfield living a short distance from New Brunswick was killed by lightning. , D
700602	A young boy named Dow, aged 12, At Union, near Keyport, died of lockjaw from stepping on a nail. , D
700602	John F. Butcher, formerly of this neighborhood, son of Samuel Butcher, dec'd, was murdered in Mandaville, Missouri, on the 2nd inst., by being shot by Abie Lee. , D
700602	Richard Stockton Field died on Wednesday. He was born in Princeton and was 67 years old at death. [Long article on his legal career.] , D
700602	William Andrews Wakely, Post Master, died at his residence on Friday, May 27th. He was 54 years old and leaves a wife, two sons and a little daughter. He was from Cranbury, NJ. , D
700609	Gen. Caldwell K. Hall died at his residence in Trenton, Monday. He was born in Philadelphia, the brother of Rev. J. Hall, and of Mrs. G. N. Abeel. , D
700609	In this borough, on the 7th inst., John S., son of John M. Dey, aged 12 years. , D
700609	James Smith threw himself in front of a train in Hackettstown last week and was killed. He leaves a wife and child in Jersey City. , D
700609	Mrs. Donohue, living at Four Mile Tank, this side of New Brunswick, was run over by a train and killed. , D
700609	On Thursday, June 9th, by Rev. J. B. Davis, James Paxton to Mrs. Sarah M. Anderson, all of Hightstown. , M
700616	At Jersey City, on the 6th inst., Ida, aged 7 years, 4 months and on the 10th inst., Sallie, aged 9 years and 8 months, daughters of Joseph and Elizabeth Erwin. , D
700616	On Sunday, June 5th, by Rev. J. S. Phelps, John R. Groves of Hightstown to Miss Julia E. Bennett, of New Brunswick. , M

Abstracts of the Deaths and Marriages in the *Hightstown Gazette*, 18 April 1861 - 28 December 1871

****

700616	On the 19th of May, at the residence of Elijah V. Perrine, Esq, by the Rev. A. L. Armstrong, Joseph Hunt, Jr., to Miss Jennie Perrine, all of Dutch Neck, NJ. , M
700616	On the 9th of May, at the Parsonage, by the Rev. A. L. Armstrong, John H. Lewis to Miss Catherine M. Davison, both of Dutch Neck, NJ. , M
700623	At Perrineville, on the 22nd inst., Mrs. Ann Perrine, in the 96th year of her age. , D
700623	Miss Sarah Cox, a young lady of Camden, died on Sunday. It is believed that she was poisoned by another lady in her boarding house, who was arrested. , D
700623	Samuel Keys, former member of the Assembly from Bordentown, died at his home in New Brunswick on Tuesday last week, of dropsy, aged about 50 years. He was employed with the C. & A. Rail Road. , D
700630	In Trenton, NJ, on the 26th inst., John W. Updike, aged 32 years. , D
700630	Mrs. Briest, wife of John Briest, Esq., editor of the "Emporium", died on Sunday. , D
700630	On the 25th inst., by his honor J. C. Johnson, Mayor, at the Saloon of D. W. Robbins, Hightstown, John W. Burck to Miss Laura Grover, both of Ocean Co.. , M
700707	A son of Mr. J.P. Doremus, of Paterson was bitten by a dog and later died from rabies. , D
700707	At Perrineville, on the 23d ult., Austin Rue, aged 59 years. , D
700707	Near Windsor, on the 29th ult., of consumption, Jonathan E. Hutchinson, aged about 40 years. , D
700707	On the 4th inst., at Pemberton, by Rev. L.D. Stultz, John L. Disbrow of South Amboy to Miss Catharine J. Van Duesen of Pemberton. , M
700707	On the 25th ult., at his residence near Hightstown, Joseph M. Taylor in the 80th year of his age. , D
700707	On Thursday, Miss Maggie King was drowned at Bordentown while bathing. , D

Abstracts of the Deaths and Marriages in the *Hightstown Gazette*, 18 April 1861 - 28 December 1871

****

700714	A little child of Samuel Kirby, living at Oceanville, fell and struck his head on Thursday, and died. , D
700714	Mr. Cooper, of Sharon, who was run over by a train, died of his injuries. , D
700721	A colored boy, named Edmund Rock and a white boy, named Sickles, aged 9 and 10 respectively, were drowned in Nesbitt's Pond, at Farmingdale, on Wednesday. , D
700721	Dr. Dayton of Matawan, died suddenly on Tuesday. His health had been failing for some time previous. , D
700721	George Gregory and his wife and a Mrs. Caldwell, a relative from Davenport, Ohio, were to cross the track at Woodbury on Saturday, when the horse became frightened by the train and ran onto the track. Both Mr and Mrs Gregory, who resided on a farm near Woodbury, were killed. Mrs. Caldwell was seriously injured and is not believed to be able to survive. , D
700721	The murder of Bridget Karsey, a former resident of Mount Holly, NJ, whose body was found in a house in Philadelphia in August 1869, will be recalled by the death of her murderer, Newton Champion, in Philadelphia county jail about a week ago. , D
700721	Yesterday, Charles Soutell of Long Branch Village went swimming and drowned. , D
700728	At Perrineville, July 13th, by Rev. D. F. Lockerby, Franklin B. Davison of Hightstown to Miss Mary V. Miller of Perrineville. , M
700728	By Elder P. Hartwell at his residence in Hopewell, NJ, July 24th, S. Smith Ege, Hopewell and Miss Sallie E. Pullen of Hightstown, daughter of Johnson Pullen. , M
700728	Mathias Kohler, a German shoemaker, residing at Sharon, accidently shot himself on Tuesday. He was a very poor man of about 33 years and leaves a wife and 6 small children. , D
700728	On the 23d inst., by J. R. C. Johnson, Esq., Charles H. Blake of Hightstown to Miss Mary E. Applegate of South Amboy. , M

Abstracts of the Deaths and Marriages in the *Hightstown Gazette*, 18 April 1861 - 28 December 1871

****

700804	A colored boy, aged about 14 years, whose first name was John, belonged at Paterson, and had lived with Theodore Hill, near Baker's Basin, for four years, was drowned near Baker's Basin, on Thursday. , D
700804	At the residence of Rev. J. E. Rue, Hightstown, July 28th, Mrs. Ann Ivins, in the 74th year of her age. , D
700804	Thomas Duff, was murdered in New Brunswick by Griffin and Mrs. Warren was implicated, at whose house the murder took place. , D
700811	Charles Reed, son of Abraham Reed, of this borough, died on Saturday last after being thrown from his manure spreader and his neck being broken. He leaves a wife. , D
700811	Ex-Senator George T. Cobb and J. Boyd Headley of Morristown, NJ, were among others killed in a train accident on Saturday, at Jerry's Run, near Sulphur Springs, Va. , D
700811	Sarah Crainheart and a man named Johnson were drowned in Cape May on Tuesday of last week. , D
700818	Two twin boys, a little over 9 years old, sons of Capt. Joseph Headley, were drowned at Waretown, on Saturday, July 30th. , D
700825	Daniel D. Denise, a citizen of Freehold, died suddenly in that village on Thursday last, aged 76 years. , D
700825	William F. Jackson was drowned in the mill pond at Jamesburg on Tuesday of last week. , D
700901	A little daughter of James Bowlin was killed by a train on the Perth Amboy and Woodbridge Rail Road, at the latter place on Friday. , D
700901	A train was on the C & A Rail Road from Cincinnati, and was passing Lawrence Station, had an accident and an old man from Vineland, named Kelly was killed. , D
700901	Miss Carrie Hopper, of Rahway, a niece of Dr. Rogers, died of injuries she sustained after she was thrown from a carriage accident at Bound Brook last Friday. , D

Abstracts of the Deaths and Marriages in the *Hightstown Gazette*, 18 April 1861 - 28 December 1871

****

700908	Near this borough on the 6th inst., infant son of T. J. Pullen, Esq., aged 3 months. , D
700908	On Sunday, William Marks, at Windsor, committed suicide by hanging himself in the barn. He was about 50 years old and his funeral was from the M.E. church in Windsor. He had been complaining of severe pains in his head for some days. , D
700916	A young lady, daughter of Mr. J. Armstead of Rhode Hall, was thrown from a horse she was riding on Friday and died from her injuries. , D
700916	At Toms River of Thursday, about 300 children were on a Sunday School trip, and were marching over a bridge over the river when it gave way. Eight of them were drowned: Maria Martin, Branchport; Ella Maple, Long Branch; Abbot Martin, Branchport; Helen M. Lane, Long Branch; Mary E. Stiles, Long Branch; Peter W. Howland, Branchport; M. H. Throckmorton, Branchport; James H. Martin, Long Branch. [Stiles and Howland were buried at the Centenary M.E. Church in Long Branch.] , D
700916	Capt. Robert Brown of Perth Amboy, Daniel Thomas of South Amboy, and Richard Strong, were killed in a boiler explosion on board the "Red Jacket". Thomas leaves a wife and four children. , D
700922	At Farmingdale, August 22, Joseph Wainright, of consumption. , D
700922	At the Red Tavern, August 23, very suddenly, Mr. Robert Johnson. , D
700922	Near Dutch Neck, on the 12th inst., of consumption, James G. Vaughn, aged 33 years 10 months and 27 days. , D
700922	Near Red Tavern, August 25th, of cholera infantum, Alice, daughter of Charles P. Mount, aged 14 months. , D
700929	At Cranbury, on the 27th, John Fisher Applegate. , D
700929	Jurist Robert C. Grier, died at his residence in Philadelphia on Monday. He was a well know citizen of Trenton and the NJ bar, from his presiding over sessions of the US Circuit Court. He was born in Cumberland Co, Pa., in 1794. , D

Abstracts of the Deaths and Marriages in the *Hightstown Gazette*, 18 April 1861 - 28 December 1871

****

700929	Near Dutch Neck, Sept 22d, of diphtheria, George A., son of Thomas and Caroline Evert, aged 6 years. , D
700929	Near Dutch Neck, Sept 23d, of diphtheria, Anna L. wife of Joseph Updike, aged 23 years. , D
700929	On Wednesday, at the Elmer Station, a young man named Nathan S. Curry, about 20, son of Abram Curry, attempted to jump on board but fell between the cars of a train passing the station, was run over and killed. , D
701006	At Dutch Neck, on the 30th ult., of diphtheria, Anna, daughter of Sexton Davis, dec., aged 15 years. , D
701006	At Plymouth, Michigan, Sept 11th, Gabriel Young, (formerly of Hightstown, NJ) aged 73 years. , D
701006	Near Dutch Neck, Sept 28th, of jaundice, Joseph, son of William Updike, aged 25 years. , D
701006	Near Hightstown, on the 28th ult., of consumption, Eleanor, wife of Stephen Anderson, aged 49 years. , D
701006	Near Hightstown, on the 3rd inst., Mary Ann, daughter of Anthony and Ednah Appleget, aged 33 years. , D
701006	Near Hightstown, Sept 14th, by Rev. Sears, Augustus M. Taylor to Harriet, eldest daughter of William M. Baker. , M
701006	October 4th, of diphtheria, Robert, son of Sexton Davis, dec., aged 3 years. , D
701006	September 27th, near Hulse's School House, a little girl, aged 12, a relative of Joseph Voorhees, was burned while attempting to start a fire with kerosene, resulting in her death. , D
701013	A notice re: the "right of dower of Ann Dillon, widow of Ezekiel Dillon, deceased..." , D
701013	Edward Lees Glew, died at his house in Newark last Friday. He was a native of Dublin. He leaves a widow but no family. , D

Abstracts of the Deaths and Marriages in the *Hightstown Gazette*, 18 April 1861 - 28 December 1871

701013   Mr. Taylor, a farmer in Morristown, was killed after being thrown from his wagon. , D

701013   Noah Van Houten, who lives near Amity, Sussex Co, buried a son last week, making it the 25 child he has lost. He has yet three living and has been married only once. , D

701020   Notice Re: the estate of William Marks, deceased of Mercer county. , D

701020   The whereabouts of Gilbert Winant, of near Milford, as been solved. He had been in Canandaigua and left for home of Sept 15th but never arrived. David K. Perrine went looking for him and found he had gone as far as Elmira and there learned that an unidentified man had been hit by a train there at about the same time of his disappearance. The body was disinterred, examined and determined to be Winant. Identification was made through his boots, which stated "Ashton, Hightstown, NJ". , D

701027   At the house of the bride's father, near Cranbury, Oct 6th, by Rev. T. C. Carman, John E. Vandusen to Miss Geogianna Davison, daughter of John D. Davison. , D

701027   On Tuesday, in Trenton, William Rosler, living on Jefferson Street, was kicked and pushed until he fell, struck his head and died. William Klemaun was charged with the crime. , D

701110   At Dutch Neck, 3d inst., of brain fever, Catharine, wife of William Walton, aged 30 years and 10 days. , D

701110   At Perrineville, on the 8th inst., of scarlet fever, Thomas, son of John Lewis, aged 10 years. , D

701110   By Rev. E.D. Stults, Nov 2d, John Proctor to Miss Ann W. Newman, all of South Amboy. , M

701110   By Rev. E.D. Stults, Nov 6th, Manuel Roberts to Miss Lizzie S. Skimins, all of South Amboy. , M

701110   In this borough, Oct 22nd, Amanda, daughter of David Cline, aged 4 weeks. , D

Abstracts of the Deaths and Marriages in the *Hightstown Gazette*, 18 April 1861 - 28 December 1871

****

701110 Near Dutch Neck, Oct 28th, Amanda, daughter of Alfred Lewis, aged 6 years. (Diphtheria) , D

701117 A man named Cossaboom was run over on Friday by a train near Manumuakin station of the West Jersey Rail Road. , D

701117 In this village, November 10th of consumption of the brain, William J., son of Martin L. and Mary Ogborn, aged 10 months. , D

701117 Near Dutch Neck, Nov. 10, of diphtheria, Helena, daughter of Zachariah and Abigail Hankins, aged 7 years. , D

701124 On the 19th inst., in this borough, Rev. John Seger, aged 85 years. [See 24 Nov issue for long history. He was born in NY City 14 Feb 1786. He married Miss Eunice Alston of NY. His 1st wife died leaving 5 children. He married (2nd) a daughter of Thomas Allen. He lost his second wife and then married Mary, the daughter of Wm. D. Jewell, who survives him.] , D

701124 Suddenly, on the 22d, in this borough, Mrs. Huldah A. Wyatt. Funeral from the residence of William Smock on Friday. , D

701124 Wm. R. Sayre, of Newark, recently committed suicide. , D

701201 In this borough, on the 27th ult., by Rev. J. S. Phelps, Abraham Gulick to Mrs. Susan Groves, all of Hightstown. , M

701201 In this borough, on the 29th ult., by S. Shangle, Esq., Clarkson Downs to Miss Catharine Boice, all of New Brunswick. , M

701201 John R. Messlor, who left Hightstown about 22 years ago, was shot through the head and beaten to death, while working on his farm at Fortville, about 20 miles from Indianapolis, Ind., on Thursday night. He was the son of Rev. V. Messlor of Monmouth, about 48 years old, and not married. His brother brought his body here and he was taken to Goshen for burial. , D

701201 Near Hightstown, on the 27th ult., of pneumonia, Jane Louisa, eldest daughter of David V. Carhart, in the 21st year of her age. , D

Abstracts of the Deaths and Marriages in the *Hightstown Gazette*, 18 April 1861 - 28 December 1871

****

701201	On Thanksgiving, Nov 24th, at the residence of the bride, by Rev. J. B. Davis, Samuel E. Chamberlin to Miss Ann M. Taylor, daughter of John Taylor, Esq. , D
701208	In Bordentown, on the 16th ult., by Rev. Joseph Greenleaf, Henry W. Deacon of Bordentown to Lydia D. Perrine of Jamesburg. , M
701208	Near Perrineville, Dec. 2d, Mrs. Mary Sherman, aged 85 years. , D
701208	On the 10th ult, by Rev. J.L. Kehoo, at the residence of E.C. Clayton, Esq., John Forman, Esq, of Freehold to M. Louisa Clayton of Manalapanville. , M
701208	On the 17th ult., by Rev. Orr, Nicholas Waln of Cream Ridge, NJ, to Ada, only daughter of the late Charles Allmendinger of Philadelphia. , M
701208	On the 24th ult, by Rev, J.L. Kehoo, William E. Rue to Julia O. Dey, both of Cranbury. , M
701208	On the 2nd ult., at the parsonage, by Rev. J. L. Kehoo, Joseph Kerr of Manalapan to Mary J. Dean of Elizabeth City. , M
701208	On the 2nd ult., at the parsonage, by Rev. J. L. Kehoo, Wyckoff Norton of Monroe to Mrs. Julia Reynolds of New Brunswick. , M
701215	On Saturday, in New Brunswick, James Barry, about 20, was burned to death in a building that caught fire. , D
701215	On the 14th ult., at the Parsonage, by Elder P. Hartwell, Philemon Waters of Hopewell to Mrs. Mary Bastow of Hightstown. , M
701229	A man named Reynolds, a brakeman on the C&A Rail Road, was killed on Tuesday by coming into contact with the bridge near Mantua. , D
701229	At the residence of the bride's father in Jamesburg on the 15th inst., by Rev. B.S. Everett, John Finlay of Hoboken, NJ to Miss Mary E. Magee, daughter of Jos. C. Magee, Esq. , M
701229	Capt. James B. Morris, died at Lawrence on Friday, Dec 16th of consumption. He was born June 28, 1842 and was in the Civil War in Artillery. , D

Abstracts of the Deaths and Marriages in the *Hightstown Gazette*, 18 April 1861 - 28 December 1871

****

701229	In the church at Quioque, Long Island, Dec 22d, by Rev. WB Reeve, father of the bride, assisted by Rev. C.F. Worrell, father of the groom, Prof. Henry M. Worrell of Hightstown, NJ to P. Fidelia Reeve, of Quioque, NY. , M
701229	Near Rhode Hall on Tuesday, Dec. 20th, by Rev. B.S. Everett, A.C. Hart of Freehold to Miss Ella Davison, daughter of James C. Davison of Rhode Hall. , M
701229	On Christmas, by Rev. O.P. Eaches, John M. Hulick of East Windsor to Miss Sarah Updike of West Windsor. , M
701229	On Christmas, by Rev. O.P. Eaches, Samuel M. Rogers of East Windsor to Miss Joanna Updike of West Windsor. , M
701229	On the 14th inst, by Rev. J. G. Symmes, Stephen J. Perrine and Miss Lydia Ann Wycoff, daughter of D. Baird Wycoff, all of Monroe. , M
701229	On the 1st inst, by Rev. J. G. Symmes, Stephen Voorhees and Miss Sarah A. Johnson, daughter of Nicholas Johnson, of Three Mile Run. , M
701229	On the 21st inst, by Rev. J. G. Symmes, Merritt M. Lewis and Miss Melvina Mount, daughter of Ezekiel Mount, all of Perrineville. , M
701229	On the 24th inst, by Rev. J. G. Symmes, John H. Schenck and Miss Emily Conover, daughter of Rutus Conover, all of Cranbury. , M
701229	On the 7th inst, by Rev. J. G. Symmes, George M. Duncan to Miss Lydia F. Johnson, daughter of Henry Johnson, all of Cranbury. , M
701229	On the 9th ult., by Rev. J. G. Symmes, W. Wilberforce Walker, of Bloomfield and Miss Anna W. Wilbur, daughter of Edward Wilbur, dec'd, of Cranbury. , M
701229	On Tuesday, Dec. 20, by Rev. O.P. Eaches, Chas. H. Lott to Miss Sarah Collier, both of New Egypt. , M
710105	At Manchester, NJ, Dec 17th, Lewis I. Holman, aged 25 years. He was a member of the Presbyterian church of Holmanville. , D

Abstracts of the Deaths and Marriages in the *Hightstown Gazette*, 18 April 1861 - 28 December 1871

****

710105	At the residence of Jos. McMurran, Hightstown, December 30, by Rev. T.B. Appleget, Symmes H. Miller of the "Gazette" office to Miss Agnes E. Ashton, daughter of Chas. Ashton, Esq., of New Egypt. , M
710105	Cranbury - William Van Horn of Van Horn and Bergen, merchants, died on Saturday last. He had been suffering from paralysis for a year or more. , D
710105	December 21st, at the house of the bride's father, near Union Valley, by Rev. J. S. Van Dyke, John H. Bawden to Miss Adelia Dey. , M
710105	December 7th, at the house of the bride's mother, in Cranbury, by Rev. J. S. Van Dyke, James S. Fisher to Miss Ella Hibbets, all of Cranbury. , M
710105	On the 23rd of November, at the parsonage, Dutch Neck, by Rev. A. L. Armstrong, Ramsey Rake to Miss Ellen Davison, all of Dutch Neck. , M
710105	On the 28th of December, by Rev. J.L. Kehoo, at the residence of the bride's parents in Monroe township, Lawrence T. Norris of Hightstown, and Miss Annie Amanda Davison. , M
710105	On the 29th of December, at the residence of John B. Vannest, by Rev. A. L. Armstrong, James V. Wyckoff to Miss Lydia C. Vannest. , M
710105	On the 31st of December, at the parsonage, by Rev. A. L. Armstrong, Franklin G. Fort to Miss Mary B., daughter of William Hooper, all of Dutch Neck. , M
710112	Dec. 29th, at the residence of the bride's father , by Rev. W. E. Greenleaf, Edwin C. Prickett of South Amboy to Miss Lizzie M., only daughter of Wm. Crammer, Esq., of Medford Township. , M
710112	Dec. 31st, at the M.E. parsonage, Allentown, by Rev. G.C. Stanger, Samuel Bozarth of Allentown, to Miss Eleanor F. Reed of Page's Corner, NJ. , M
710119	In this borough, on the 10th inst., Ellen Rue, of scarlet fever, aged 8 years. , D
710119	Near Milford, Jan. 17th, of consumption, Daniel Johnes, aged 52 years, 2 months. , D

Abstracts of the Deaths and Marriages in the *Hightstown Gazette*, 18 April 1861 - 28 December 1871

****

710119	On Thursday, an inquest was held over the body of Osker Scheibe, the German who was shot by Timothy Coogan on Dec. 24th in South Amboy. , D
710126	At Hightstown, on the 19th inst., by Rev. J. B. Davis, assisted by Rev. J. G. Symmes, Forman P. Wetherill of Allentown, NJ to Miss Sadie A. Dey, daughter of David B. Dey, Esq., of Hightstown. , M
710126	On Wednesday, Jan 18th, at the residence of Joseph Coleman, Esq., Dutch Neck, by Rev. O.P. Eaches, assisted by Rev. Armstrong, Geo. E. Snedeker to Miss Adaline E. Mount. , M
710126	On Wednesday, Jan 18th, by Rev. J. B. Davis, Theodore Tindall of West Windsor to Miss Mary Y. Applegate, daughter of John A. Applegate, Esq. , M
710126	The trial of Walter Griffin for the murder of Thomas Duff last July began in New Brunswick on Tuesday. , D
710202	At the residence of the bride's father, near Cranbury, on the 26th ult., by Rev. T.C. Carmen, assisted by J. S. Van Dyke, William D. Perrine of Monroe to Miss Sarah Matilda Ely, daughter of Jos. J. Ely, Esq. , M
710202	Geo. W. Davison, of Perrineville, died at his residence last week after a brief illness. He was a member of the Perrineville Church. , D
710202	In this borough, Jan. 30th, Abraham Vannest, in the 72d year of his age. , D
710202	In this borough, on the 30th ult., Mrs. Mary Edwards, widow of Samuel Edwards, dec'd, in the 76th year of her age. , D
710202	On the 19th ult., by Rev. Jos. G. Symmes, John Edgar Stults and Miss Sarah Elizabeth Stults, daughter of T. Saulter Stults, all of Cranbury. , M
710202	On the 19th ult., by Rev. Jos. G. Symmes, Wm. D. Silver of South Amboy and Miss Kate Gulick, daughter of Dr. S. Gulick. , M
710202	On the 26th ult., at the residence of the bride's father, by Rev. I. H. Willmarth, C. Calvin Groves, of Hightstown to Miss Rebecca G. Ewan, daughter of J. Ewan of Pemberton. , M

Abstracts of the Deaths and Marriages in the *Hightstown Gazette*, 18 April 1861 - 28 December 1871

****

710202	On the 29th of December, at the parsonage of Leesburg, by the Rev. W.B. Vanleer, Jeremiah C. Morris to Miss Roda M. Vanleer, daughter of the officiating clergyman. , M
710209	At the residence of Henry Merrill, the bride's brother, in Brooklyn, NY, on the 2d inst, by Rev. J. S. Phelp, Wm. T. Brown of Hightstown, NJ to Miss Ellen Merrill of Williamstown, NJ. , M
710209	Feb 1st, by Rev. William M. Wells, at the residence of the bride, William Huff of Blue Ball to Miss Sophie M. Smith of Jamesburg. , M
710209	John Tieman and John Doran, watchmen, were run over and killed at New Brunswick by a passing freight train. , D
710209	On the 26th of January, at the residence of Amos Tindal, Esq., near Edinburg, by Rev. A.L. Armstrong, Thomas Hooper to Miss Amy Tindall, eldest daughter of Amos Tindall, Esq. , M
710209	On the 31st ult., Samuel M. Pul[l]en to Miss Maggie H. Moore, both of Hightstown, NJ. , M
710216	Geo. W. Fielder, whose death we announce in another section, was the senior member of Fielder, Mount & Jimeson. Funeral at the M.E. church, Hightstown. , D
710223	Charles Whittick, formerly of this borough, has died from the wounds he received in the war for the Union. He is now of Burlington, NJ. He was with Co. A, 6th Reg., NJ Vols. , D
710223	Feb. 18th, by Rev. C. F. Worrell, at New Bedford, Sidney Smith of South Amboy to Miss Gertrude S. Thompson, of Leedsville, NJ. , M
710223	Henry Glenbudd, a colored man, was killed on Monday, near Englishtown. While jumping from a moving car to the engine tender, he fell under the wheels. , D
710223	In this borough, on Monday, February 13th, of congestion of the lungs, Johnnie Davis, infant son of Stephen and Mary E. Morris. , D
710223	Near this borough, on the 22nd inst., of bronchitis, Mary E., wife of Peter H. Danser. Funeral services at the Presbyterian Church, Hightstown. , D

Abstracts of the Deaths and Marriages in the *Hightstown Gazette*, 18 April 1861 - 28 December 1871

****

710302	A colored boy, named Azariah Bolles, aged 16, was run over on Sunday last by a train, while working with a gang on the track. , D
710302	Dr. Evan Dudley, a native of Moorestown, Burlington County was found dead in his bed at Philadelphia a few days since. He died from an overdose of morphine. , D
710302	Feb 25th, by Charles H. Perrine, Justice of the Peace, Luther Boyce to Miss Hannah M. Bysson, all of Monroe Township, Middlesex County, NJ. , M
710302	John Ware, found guilty of the murder of is father in Camden Courts, has been sentenced to be hung on the 10th of April next. , D
710302	L.B. Randolph of Manchester, Ocean County, was arrested on bigamy. He obtained a divorce from his wife in December in Connecticut and married the daughter of Mrs. Wyckoff of Manchester. The divorce was set aside as illegal. , M
710302	On Sunday last, a little boy, 2 or 3 years old, a son of David Hankinson, near Squan Village, was drowned in the creek behind the house. , D
710302	Thomas Carhart, a citizen of Keyport, died suddenly on the 25th, at the age of 83 years. , D
710309	At Dutch Neck, 3rd inst., John F. Mount, aged 28 years, 9 months and 16 days. , D
710309	In South Brunswick township, on the 1st inst., Stella, daughter of Edward and Carrie H. Lucas. , D
710309	In this borough, on the 2d inst., Mrs. Groves Gulick, in the 64th year of her age. , D
710309	Near Danley's Mills, Feb 25th, Richard Ely, ged 75 years. , D
710309	Near Milford, 1st inst., Kenneth Holman, aged 89 years. , D
710316	Mrs. Jacob Walker, of New Brunswick, committed suicide by shooting on Sunday. , D
710316	On the 1st inst., by Rev. H. Watson, Benjamin Richardson to Miss Hannah Dey. , M

Abstracts of the Deaths and Marriages in the *Hightstown Gazette*, 18 April 1861 - 28 December 1871

****

710316	On the 5th inst., at the residence of Mr. Whitlock, by Rev. J. S. Phelps, John Ewart to Miss Amanda Baremore, all of Hightstown, NJ. , M
710316	On Wednesday, March 15th, by Rev. J. B. Davis, Henry F. Edsall to Miss Jennie A. Rue, all of Hightstown, NJ. , M
710316	Samuel Kay, proprietor of the Untied States Hotel, died at his residence in State St [Trenton], yesterday. , D
710316	Suddenly, on the 6th inst., near Red Tavern, of heart disease, Abby Dey, aged 60 years. , D
710323	In this borough, on the 14th inst., Abigail S., daughter of Howard Ashton, aged 1 year and 5 months. , D
710330	At the parsonage, Dutch Neck, by Rev. A. L. Armstrong, on the 22d inst., Gerardus W. Wiley to Miss Sarah Ann Hart, both of Pennington, NJ. , M
710330	On the 27th inst., at Cranbury, Charles Edgar, son of Derrick and Sarah F. Hoagland, aged 7 months and 20 days. , D
710330	On the 3rd, inst., Frenchtown, NJ, a daughter of Henry W. Miller, of that place, who is "not all bright", aged "some twenty years", lit some matches and caught herself on fire. She was rescued and survived. In the meantime, her brother Arthur, aged 4, got into some morphine upstairs that was left out and died from the dose. , D
710406	At the parsonage, Squan Village, by Rev. E.D. Stults, on April 2d, Mr. Henry Wainwright to Miss Addie V. Brown, youngest daughter of Capt. John M. Brown. All of Squan Village. , M
710406	In this borough, March 31st, Clark H. Silvers, aged 66 years. , D
710406	In this borough, Thursday morning, April 6th, of Consumption, Mrs. Mary E., wife of Rev. S. Morris, aged 33 years. , D
710406	Near Milford, March 30th, of Cancer, John Perrine, aged 58 years. , D
710413	At Plainsboro, on the 10th inst., Martha, wife of Arthur Ruding, and youngest daughter of the late Israel Pearce, Esqr. , D

Abstracts of the Deaths and Marriages in the *Hightstown Gazette*, 18 April 1861 - 28 December 1871

****

710413	On the 5th inst., by the Rev. Joseph G. Symmes, Mr. James Harkness of Princeton, to Miss Cornelia Lanning, daughter of the late Nathaniel Lanning of Cranbury. , M
710420	In this borough, on the 18th inst., John Compton in the 75th year of his age. , D
710420	In this borough, on the 6th inst., Henry, infant son of Patrick Mc Gowan, aged 14 months. , D
710427	At Perrineville, April 20th, 1871, by Rev. D.F. Lockerby, at the residence of Mr. Samuel Rue, Joseph C. Magee of Jamesburg, to Eleanor B. Perrine, of Perrineville. , M
710427	At the Parsonage, Perrineville, by Rev. D.F. Lockerby, April 2d, 1871, Clayton Crammer, of Cassville, to Charlotte Davis of Millstone, Monmouth county, N.J. , M
710427	On the 16th inst., also at the Parsonage, Perrineville, by the Rev. D.F. Lockerby, Charles C. McCoy of Cream Ridge, to Margaret E. Dey of Brooklyn. L.I. , M
710504	On the 20th ult., in the Third Presbyterian Church of Trenton, by the Rev. Samuel M. Studdiford, William Austin Vescelieus to Phoebe A., daughter of the late Wesley Danser, of Trenton. , M
710518	Annie Corbett, servant, at Trenton dies from burns. , D
710608	At the Union Church, Squan Village, on the 4th inst., Mr. James Johnson to Miss Emma J. Gifford, all of Ocean county, N.J. , M
710608	Near Hightstown, on the 2d inst., of Neuralgia, Israel Vaughn, aged 74 years. , D
710608	Near Vanhise's corner, on the 3d inst., Albert, son of Alfred Lewis, aged 8 months. , D
710622	By Rev. H. Watson, June 18th, Mr. Henry Hanes, of Phila. "Post", to Miss Susanna Adams of Pleasantville, N.J. , M
710622	By Rev. H. Watson, on May 27, Mr. J. K. Andrews to Miss A. E. Price, all of Pleasantville. , M

Abstracts of the Deaths and Marriages in the *Hightstown Gazette*, 18 April 1861 - 28 December 1871

****

710622	Near Milford, on the 15th inst., Hendrickson Wright, of Consumption, aged 38 years. , D
710622	Near this place, on the 18th inst., Elias Tice, of old age, aged 73 years. , D
710629	At St. Paul's Church, Rahway, N.J., on the 27th inst., by Rev. Mr. Pettit of Bordentown, Mr. W. W. Swett to Miss Harriet Stults, both of Hightstown. , M
710629	Col. John I. Conover died recently at the residence of his son, J. Nelson Conover, in Manalapan. He was in his 87th year. , D
710629	Near Allentown, June 22d, Susan Borden, of heart disease. , D
710629	Tuesday evening, June 29th, by Rev. Wm. M. Stanleup, Mr. John W. Truax to Miss Anna E. Peters, all of the city of Camden. , M
710706	At Hightstown, on the Fourth of July, by Hon. J. C. Norris, Mayor of the borough, Mr. David Mosher to Miss Isabella Smith, both of Wrightstown. , M
710706	At his residence in Cranbury, on the 5th inst., of Bright's disease of the Kidneys, George Farr, aged 50 years. The funeral services will be held in the Second Presbyterian Church, Cranbury, at 11 o'clock on Saturday morning, July 8th. [Larger obit in the 13 July issue re: George Farr, Sheriff of Middlesex County.] , D
710713	In New Egypt, on July 10th., Charles D., son of Ross H. Copperwait, aged 10 years, drowned. , D
710713	In Philadelphia, on July 8th, Joseph H., son of Robert Purdy, aged 1 year. , D
710713	In this borough, on July 1st, Wallace, son of James Baremore, aged 4 months. , D
710713	Near Milford, on July 2d, Gershom Cottrell, aged 58 years. , D
710720	Mr. John Mount, of Squan Village, died on Monday, after several months of terrible suffering from cancer on his face. , D
710727	July 13th, at Penn's Neck, of Sunstroke, William Case, aged 50 years. , D
710803	At Allentown, July 31st, Lydia, wife of Isaac Rogers. , D

Abstracts of the Deaths and Marriages in the *Hightstown Gazette*, 18 April 1861 - 28 December 1871

****

710803	In Hamilton Township, near Sandhills, Mrs. Ann Wilson, of palsy, aged 77 years. , D
710810	A young man by the name of Gill was killed by the cars at Windsor, on Tuesday night. He had become overpowered by the Harvest Home, and was sitting down on the track when the eleven o'clock come along and struck him. [In the next issue, the paper said the name was not Gill, it was Connolly. It also stated that the "Harvest Home" had not gotten the best of him.] , D
710810	Died in this borough, August 4th, of Consumption, Sarah Applegate, aged 39 years. , D
710824	At Cranbury, on the 2nd inst., Mrs. Jane Blane Cole. , D
710824	In this borough, on the 19 inst., of Consumption, Mrs. Rebecca Baremore, wife of James Baremore, aged 42 years. , D
710824	On the 5th inst., by the Rev. Wm. M. Stanleup, Mr. John Wilson, of Haddonfield, to Miss Mary Peters of Camden, NJ. , M
710831	In this borough, Sept. 30th, Cornelia, daughter of Mr. David Van Marter, in the 26th year of her age. Funeral services at the M.E. Church, on Friday morning at 10 1/2 o'clock. Friends will meet at the house at 10 o'clock. , D
710831	Near Union Valley, on the 26th inst., of Summer Complaint, Harry, son of William Lot, aged 6 months. , D
710831	Thursday, Aug. 24th, 1871, by Rev. O.P. Eaches, Mr. John H. Grover to Miss Margaret A. Ireland, both of Imlaystown. , M
710907	James Thompson, of Cranbury, while walking on the railroad track at Monmouth Junction, on Wednesday afternoon, was run over by the Washington Express train and instantly killed. , D
710907	Rebecca Rue, widow of William Rue, died at Perrineville, Monmouth Co, NJ, August 12th 1871. [There is a good long obituary regarding her maiden name of Holeman. She was born 18 May 1777, her sister was Anna Perrine, etc. Photos of these two sisters in their old age can be found in the Hightstown-East Windsor Historical Society collections.] , D

Abstracts of the Deaths and Marriages in the *Hightstown Gazette*, 18 April 1861 - 28 December 1871

****

710921	At Manalapan, September 20th, by Rev. A.P. Cobb, Mr. Charles E. Teale of Brooklyn, N.Y. to Mrs. Lida McChesney, daughter of Robt. R. McChesney, of Manalapan. , M
710921	At the residence of the bride's father, near Cranbury, on Wednesday, September 13th, by Rev. T. C. Carman, Mr. George Perrine to Miss Anna V. Ervin, daughter of Mr. George Ervin. , M
710921	In Cranbury, on the 18th inst., of Consumption, Jane Ann, only daughter of John S. and Mary Davison, aged 28 years. , D
710921	In this borough, Sept. 20th, of Consumption, Lydia Ann, wife of Embley Pullen, in the 41st year of her age. , D
710921	On the 14th inst., by Rev. J. B. Davis, Mr. Marsena Riggs to Miss Anna P. West, all of Hightstown. , M
711005	At Rocky Hill, on the 2d inst., Wm. Perrine, of consumption. , D
711005	At the M.E. Parsonage, Hightstown, by Rev. J. S. Phelps, Oct. 1st, Mr. Wm. Gilliland, to Miss Emma F. Roberts, both of Rhode Hall, N.J. , M
711005	At the residence of the bride's father on September 28, 1871, by the Rev. T. C. Carman, Mr. Vincent Hughes to Miss Lizzie Nutt, daughter of Mr. Samuel Nutt, all of Cranbury, N.J. , M
711005	Died in Old Bridge, 21 Sept 1871, Newton Conover, of sunstroke which led to consumption. , D
711005	In this borough, on the 3d inst., Merriet Lewis, aged 23 years. Funeral services at the Baptist Church, Hightstown, tomorrow (Friday) morning at 11 o'clock. , D
711005	John L. Lewis and his son Merriet were digging a drain from the Baptist Institute to the pond when the trench caved in killing the son, aged 23, leaving a wife. He was a member of the Perrineville Presbyterian Church. , D
711012	On Saturday, October 7th, 1871, by Rev. O.P. Eaches, Mr. Stephen Cathcart, of West Windsor, to Miss Elizabeth Wilson of Hightstown. , M

Abstracts of the Deaths and Marriages in the *Hightstown Gazette*, 18 April 1861 - 28 December 1871

****

711019	At Flushing, L.I., Sept. 20, by Rev. E. S. Fairchild, Mr. George J. Ely, of Hightstown, to Miss Elizabeth Jane, daughter of C. H. Rusher of the former place. , M
711019	At the M.E. Parsonage, Pemberton, NJ, on Tuesday, Oct 17th, 1871, by Rev. P. Cline, (Rev. Geo. K. Morris of Salem assisting), Rev. C. F. Garrison, of the N.J. Conference, to Miss Hannah S. Cline, daughter of the officiating clergyman. , M
711026	On the evening of Oct. 19th, at the residence of the bride's parents in Laurel street, Bridgeton, by Rev. H. Watson of Egg Harbor, Mr. Abram Robinson to Miss Harriet Jaggers, both of Bridgeton, NJ. , M
711026	On the evening of Sept 12, 1871, by Rev. H. Watson, Mr. Constant Adams to Mrs. Eliza Kears, all of Bakersville, Atlantic Co, NJ. , M
711102	At Hightstown, on the 25th inst., by Rev. J. S. Phelps, Mr. George McCabe, of Freehold, to Miss Nancy Thompson, of Clarksburg. , M
711102	At Manalapan, Oct. 27th, of Inflammation of the bowels, Mrs. Louisa, wife of Wm. Halsted, of Muscatine, Iowa, aged 27 years. , D
711102	By the Rev. Joseph G. Symmes, on the 19th ult., Mr. Wm. H. Neary to Miss Caroline Lake, daughter of Mr. Oliver Lake. , M
711102	By the Rev. Joseph G. Symmes, on the 8th ult., Mr. Cornelius Vleit to Miss Frances Chrisman, daughter of Mr. John Chrisman, dec'd. , M
711102	John J. Errickson, about 19, murdered in a pool hall fight in Freehold, NJ , D
711102	Oct 8th, by Rev. W.B. Vanleer, Mr. Geo. H. Newman to Miss Ruth A. Morton, all of Wall township, Monmouth county. , M
711109	In Cranbury, Nov 1st, 1871, Miss Sallie Newton, aged 80 years. , D
711109	In this borough, on the 6th inst., of consumption, Dr. J. N. Fairbank, aged 47 years. [There is a larger article in the same issue of the paper.] , D
711116	On the 24th of August, by the Rev. A. L. Armstrong, at the Parsonage, Dutch Neck, NJ, Mr. John H. Johnson of Princeton Basin, to Miss Emma J. Lake, daughter of Mr. Oliver Lake of South Brunswick, NJ. , M

Abstracts of the Deaths and Marriages in the *Hightstown Gazette*, 18 April 1861 - 28 December 1871

****

711116	On the 24th of August, by the Rev. A. L. Armstrong, at the Parsonage, Dutch Neck, NJ, Mr. Martin Johnson of Princeton Basin, to Miss Alice A. Lake, daughter of Mr. Oliver Lake of South Brunswick, NJ. , M
711130	At Hopewell, NJ on Saturday 15th inst., Sarah, wife of Mr. Smith Ege, and daughter of Mr. Johnson Pullen of Hightstown. , D
711130	At the residence of the bride's father, on the 26th inst., by Rev. J. S. Phelps, Mr. William S. Adams of Trenton, to Miss Jane Soden of Hightstown, NJ. , M
711130	On 28th inst., of diphtheria, George, son of Mr. Mulford Norris, aged 7 years. Funeral on Friday morning. To meet at the house 10 1/2 o'clock. Services at the Baptist church, Hightstown at 11 o'clock. , D
711207	On the evening of the 22d. ult., at the residence of the bride's parents, by Rev. J. Temple Rowe, of Philadelphia, assisted by Rev. T. Taylor Heiss of Barnsboro, NJ, and Rev. J. Karcher of Reading, PA, William Lyne to Sallie A. Becker, both of Philadelphia. , M
711207	Peter F. Runyon, the oldest Justice of Middlesex, died in New Brunswick, on Friday, aged 85 years. , D
711214	At Cedar Bridge, by Rev. E.D. Stults, Nov 21st., Mr David E. Cook to Miss Jane Truex, all of Ocean county. , M
711214	At the M.E. Parsonage, Cranbury, by Rev. T. C. Carman, on Nov 28th, Mr. Enoch W. Hart of Cranbury to Miss Ella K. Whitemore of Pittsburg, PA. , M
711214	At the M.E. Parsonage, Oct 8, 1871, by Rev. E.D. Stults, Mr. Abram Carlock of Monmouth Co., to Miss Louisa Havins of Ocean Co, NJ. , M
711214	At the Parsonage, Squan Village, by Rev. E.D. Stults, Nov 28th., Mr. Elisha Tilton to Miss Mary Ann Chasa, all of Monmouth Co. , M
711214	At White Hill, Eveline, daughter of Grandon Reed, aged 11 weeks. , D
711214	By Rev. E.D. Stults, near Squan Bridge, at the house of the bride, Mr James J. Allen of Monmouth Co, to Miss Mary A. Allen of Ocean Co, NJ. , M

Abstracts of the Deaths and Marriages in the *Hightstown Gazette*, 18 April 1861 - 28 December 1871

****

711214	In this borough, on the 3d inst., of Asthma, Mr. Elias Jimeson, aged 60 years. , D
711214	Near Petersburg, VA, Oct 17th, Mrs. Sarah Hance, wife of Rev. Wm. Hance, in the 54th year of her age. , D
711214	Near Smithville, on the 11th inst., of Consumption, Mrs. Jane Lanning, aged 74 years. , D
711214	Thomas E. Gravatt, post master of Clarksburg, died of lockjaw resulting from a splinter he had in his hand. , D
711221	At 12 o'clock, Thursday night, 14th inst., at Barnsboro, of diphtheria James Robinson, son of Rev. Wm. and Sarah Jane Sharp, aged 5 years and 11 months , D
711221	At Jamesburg, Dec 14, by Rev. B.S. Everett, Mr Thomas E. Perrine to Miss Hattie E., daughter of Joseph C. Magee, all of the above place. , M
711221	At Jamesburg, Dec 14, by Rev. B.S. Everett, Stephen E. Thompson of Freehold, to Miss Mary E., daughter of Edmond Rue, Esq., of Jamesburg. , M
711221	At the residence of the bride, near West Freehold, NJ, on the 14th inst., by Rev. H.B. Beegle, assisted by Rev. A. J. Gregory, John D. Beegle, son of the officiating minister to Miss Tillie Applegate. , M
711221	On the 31st inst., at Barnsborough, of diphtheria and croup, Sarah Elizabeth, daughter of Rev. Wm. and Sarah Jane Sharp, aged 3 years, 1 month and 25 days. , D
711228	On the 13th inst., by the Rev. A. L. Armstrong, at the residence of the bride's father, Mr. John H. Ely to Miss Lydia Helen, daughter of Ezekiel Wilson, M.D., all of West Windsor , M
711228	On the 20th inst., by Rev. A. L. Armstrong, at the residence of the bride's father, Mr. Charles S. Rogers to Miss Emma, oldest daughter of Mr. J. Bergen Vannest, all of West Windsor. , M

INDEX

A

Abeel: G.N., Mrs., 86
Abrahams: John, dec'd, 19; Peter M., 36; Sarah E., Miss, 19; Wm., 36
Acton: E.A., Capt., 13
Adams: Constant, 105; John B., 86; Lizzie, 43; Susanna, Miss, 101; William S., 106
Alexander: Anna Mary, Miss, 63; J.E., Rev., 40, 63, 74; James, 62; Samuel M., 40
Allen: Charles M., 49, 83; Charles S., Lt., 13; Cornelia, 28; David, 64, 82; Eliza, Miss, 55; James P., 55; James. J., 106; Laura, 28; Leyman, 77; Mary, 64; Mary A., Miss, 106; Melvina F., 83; Nathan, 76; Thomas, 93; William, 28
Allmendinger: Ada, 94; Charles, dec'd, 94
Alston: Eunice, Miss, 93
Altick: D., Mr., 79; Mattie [Hattie?], 79
Ancelin: Francis L., 66; Sarah Jane, widow, 66
Anderson: Abijah A., 66; Carrie M., Miss, 42; David, 12, 42; Edward S., 32; Eleanor, 91; Garret, 32; Garrett, 32; George, 63; Henry A., 29; Jacob, 42; James, Capt., 83; Jennie, Miss, 65; John V., 15; Joseph, 29; Matthias, 32; Samuel, 24; Sarah M., Mrs., 86; Stephen, 91; Theodore, 6, 26, 27
Andrews: J.K., Mr., 101
Androulus: Charles, 54
Appleby: Mary E., 21
Applegate: Abbie S., Miss, 56; Abijah, 55; Abijah J., 56; Alice Ann, Mrs., 47; Andrew, 71; Andrew I., 32; Anna V., Miss, 68; Anna, Miss, 5; Anthony, 56; Armenia, 22; Baird, 42; Baird W., 22; Charles H., 68; Daniel D., 79; Disbrow, 79; E. T. R., Maj., 11; Elias D., 8; Elizabeth, 71; Forman, 30; George, 38, 68; George S.H., 13; Herbert W., 59; James Henry, 22; James M., 32; James Mortimore, 78; John, 5, 23; John A., 64; John A., Esq., 97; John Fisher, 90; Kate E., Miss, 22; Lizzie, Miss, 23; Louisa, Miss, 45, 68; Magie S., 79; Margaret Ann, Miss, 42; Mary E., Miss, 88; Mary Y., Miss, 97; Peter W., 47; Richard, 11; Sarah, 103; Sarah J., Miss, 56; Thomas F., 30; Tillie, Miss, 107; Vanzant, 39; W., 68
Appleget: Adrian, Lt., 27; Anthony, 91; Ednah, 91; Gertrude A., Miss, 17; John B., Esq., 82; Mary Ann, 91; T.B., Rev., 96; Thomas B., Intro; Wille D., 82; Wm. S., 71
Archer: Joseph, 74
Archibald: Anna Jane, Miss, 81; Stewert, 81
Arms: S.E., Dr., 82
Armstead: J., Mr., 90
Armstrong: A.L., Rev., 4, 6, 9, 15, 20, 21, 22, 38, 41, 46, 53, 57, 58, 64, 65, 66, 67, 68, 70, 72, 76, 87, 96, 98, 100, 105, 106, 107; Calvin, 14; Rev., 97; Walter, Esq., 66
Arose: Jeremiah, 48
Ashton: A.J., 47, 74; Abigail S., 100; Agnes E., 96; Catherine, 47; Charles, 51; Chas., Esq., 96; Howard, 100
Atkinson: Rebecca, 12
Atwood: Jos., Rev., 45; Joseph, Rev., 41, 42, 54
Auten: Frederick P., Dr., 77
Ayres: Adelaide, 18; Elwood B., 45; Enos, 12; Gilbert V., 66; Helen, 12; Mary S., 77; Robert, 84; Samuel, 48; Stout, 77; Willard, 48; William S., 6

INDEX

B

Babbitt: P. Teller, Rev., 15
Babcock: Orville, 9
Bacon: Mattie [Hattie?], J., Mrs., 79
Badgeley: Oliver, Rev., 16
Baird, 52
Baker: Harriet, 91; Joseph, 82; Richard, 82; Sarah H., Miss, 76; William M., 91
Baldwin: Edward, 83; Hannah A., Miss, 42; Israel, 42; Wm., 83
Ballard: A.E., Rev., 58
Ballou: Hosea, Rev., 62
Bamford: James, 19
Bampton: Richard, 1
Barclay: Isaiah D., 6
Baremore: Amanda, Miss, 100; James, 64, 102, 103; Mary J., 64; Rebecca, Mrs., 103; Wallace, 102
Barker: E.B., Rev., 16; E.M., Rev., 36; James, 5; Joseph, 82; Mary, 5; Miss, 2; Richard, 5, 16, 26, 27, 36, 82
Barricklo: Amanda, Miss, 71
Barry: James, 94
Bartlett: William Alvin, Rev., 58
Bastow: Edward M., 24; John, 54; Mary, Mrs., 94
Batten: Edward, 61
Bawden: John H., 96
Bayard: James, 41; Willie, 41
Beegle: H.B., Rev., 107; John D., 107
Beekman: John V.D., 49; Mary, Miss, 70
Beers: Nelson, 85
Beisler: J.S., Rev., 58
Becker: Sallie A., 106
Bennett: Isaac S., 23; Julia E., Miss, 86; Winchester T., 35
Bergen: Ann A., Miss, 58; Charles W., 75; Eliza S., Miss, 58; G.B., 50; Gertrude, 64; James M., 75; Peter I., 28; William E., 43; Wm. G., 58
Betchner: Jacob, 81
Billings: Isaac, 50
Bilyeu: Annie, Miss, 61; Marie, Mrs, widow, 44; Peter, Sr., 44
Bishop: Capt., 46
Black: Martha, Miss, 57
Blackwell: Isaac V.D., 32; Wm. H., 32
Blake: Alfred, 11, 31; Charles H., 88; Price P., 33; Ruth, Mrs., 64; Thomas, 33
Blavelt: J.S., Esq., 79
Bloodgood: Jackson, 13
Bodine: Elizabeth, Widow, 24; Lydia Ann, 43; Peter, 43; Vincent, 45
Boice: Catharine, Miss, 93
Bolles: Azariah, 99
Booream: Cornelius, 29
Borden: Enoch R, Esq., 85; Susan, 102
Bottles: William J., 80
Boud: Charles H., 44
Bowker: Charles, 79
Bowlin: James, 89
Bowne: Carrie A., Miss, 74; Henry, 29; Jennie A., Miss, 44; Maria, Mrs., 29
Boyce: Luther, 99
Boyd: Charles, 20
Bozarth: Samuel, 96
Bradley: James, 50; John, 50
Brandt: Charles, 2; Richard, 2
Bransert: Frederick, 74; John, 74
Brant: Corp., 14
Briest: John, Esq., 87; Mrs., 87
Britton: Abraham, 66; Isaac, 69
Brocaw: Thomas, 78
Brokaw: Isaac, 40; Mary, Miss, 40
Brophy: Mrs., 50
Brower: David, 27; Jennie L., Miss, 52
Browers: Daniel, 70
Brown: Addie V., Miss, 100; Charles F., 73;

INDEX

Daniel, 5; Elias, 8; Elizabeth T., 85;
G.F., 47; George G., 45; George W.,
20; H.M., Rev., 12, 13; Jane A., 4;
Jesse, 20; John, 78; John M., Capt.,
100; John W., 42; Lizzie, Miss, 41;
Maggie, Miss, 59; Margaret, 62;
Nelson, 62; Rahselah M., 30; Randall,
19; Robert, Capt., 90; Samuel, 70;
Taylor, 85; William E., 23; Wm. T., 98

Browne: C.C., Mr., 74
Brownell: Josephine M.L., Miss, 15
Buckalew: F. Lemuel, 75; James, 72
Budd: Benjamin, 5; Emeline, 5; Emily,,Mrs., 20
Bunting: Christianna, 54; Louisa, Miss, 55
Burck: John W., 87
Burdell: Dr., 70
Burke: Elmira, Miss, 7
Burkly: Franklin, 29
Burns: Emma, 65; Stephen, 11, 25, 27; Thomas, 53
Burt: Jacob O., 35; James C., 35
Burtis: Louisa S., Miss, 19; Sallie L., Miss, 42
Butcher: John F., 86; John, Esq., 14; Samuel, 57; Samuel, dec'd, 86
Butterfield: I., Rev., 18, 19, 20, 21, 22, 23, 24
Byard: Charles H., 38
Bysson: Hannah, Miss, 99

C

Cabrin: Mr., 83
Caldwell: Mrs., 88
Caminade: Nettie, 37; Samuel, 37
Camless: Robert, 40
Campbell: Daniel H., colored, 85; J.K., Rev., 69
Canleer: Roda M., Miss, 98
Cannon: Ella S., Miss, 75; Gov., 75
Capner: Mary Lavinia, Miss, 72

Car: Thomas, 41
Carhart: David K., 93; Jane Louisa, 93; Thomas, 99
Carlock: Abram, 106
Carman: J.C., Rev., 79; John D., 29; T.C., Rev., 49, 66, 70, 77, 81, 82, 83, 92, 104, 106
Carmen: Alfred, 29; John, 29; T.C., Rev., 67, 97
Carmichael: I.W., 24; Rachel W., 85
Carr: A.H., Esq., 78; Elisha, 59; Ella S., Rev., 78; James, 11, 26, 27
Carson: James, 9
Case: William, 102
Cathcart: George W., 29; Stephen, 104
Chamberlain: Addison, 18; Alfred, 7; John, 68; Joseph, 18; Mary E., 16; Sarah M., Miss, 6
Chamberlin: A.E., 23; Abijah J., 24, 65; Abijah L., 45; Ann, Mrs., 45; Emma, 48; Julia, 61; Lizzie, 54; Randolph, 54; Samuel E., 94; Thomas, 48; Thomas M., 61
Champion: Newton, 88
Chandler: F., Rev., 74; Lymna A., Hon., 15
Chaplain: J.F., Rev., 75
Chasa: Mary Anna, Miss, 106
Chase: L., Rev., 55, 56; L., Rev., 60, 64, 65, 68; R.G., Rev., 50; Rev., 66; Sarah D., Miss, 58; Walter H., 57
Cheeseman: Henry, 15; Sarah, 15
Chrisman: Frances, Miss, 105; John, dec'd, 105
Clark: Benjamin, Esq., 46; John, 1; Mary B., Miss, 46; Silas W., 44; Susan, 47; Susan Johnes, Mrs., 56; William, 4
Clarke: Lydia, Miss, 2
Clayton: Abraham J., 40; Alfred, 1; Cyrenius T., 77; David Gordon, 53; David, Sr., 34; E.C., Esq., 94; M. Louisa, 94; William, 34
Cline: Amanda, 92; David, 92; Elizabeth S., 27;

INDEX

Hannah S., Miss, 105; P. Rev., 43; P., Rev., 26, 27, 38, 44, 47, 54, 55, 105; Phillip, Rev., 58; Rev., 54

Cobb: A.P., Rev., 104; George T., Ex-Senator, 89

Cochran: J., Rev., 24

Cole: Edwina, Miss, 78; Enoch K., 42; Francis W., 47; George A., 52; James C., 67; Jane Blane, Mrs., 103; Jesse R., 14; Thomas, 40; W.J., 56; William W., 28; Williard S., 77; Wm. Jones, 28

Coleman: Anthony, 11; Christia, 55; Emma J., Miss, 67; Isaac Pearson, Dr., 76; Jesse, 67; Joseph, Esq., 97

Coleman, Esq.: J.B., 55

Collier: Sarah, Miss, 95

Combs: Dorothea A., Miss, 76

Compton: Hannah, 79; John, 30, 101; Lewis, 41; Tobias, 10

Connell: Thomas, 85

Connelly: Bernard, Jr., 81; J.P., Rev., 19, 39

Connett: Amos, 65

Connolly, 103: John C. S., 5

Conover: David L., 83; Ebenezer, 63; Edward, 70; Elias R., 38; Emily, Miss, 95; Geo. W., 34; George W., 32; Hannah, 54; J. Nelson, 102; James, 4; John E., 32; John I., Col., 102; Martha E., Miss, 45; Newton, 104; Peter, 32, 34; Peter H., 73, 74; R. Baxter, 18; Runey, 23

Conover: Rutus, 95

Conover: Sarah Ann, Miss, 21; Thomas J., 32, 34; Ussie, Miss, 20; Vincent, 68; Wm. V., 32

Coogan: Timothy, 97

Cook: Adalaide E., 52; Adelaide, Miss, 15; David E., 106; James, Gen., 7; Libby D., Miss, 19; Margaret, Mrs., 7

Cookman: Alfred, Rev., 74

Cooley: Sarah, Miss, 45

Coolley: Albert, 25, 27

Cooper: John O., 64; Mr., 88

Copperwait: Charles D., 102; Ross H., 102

Corbett: Annie, 101

Coriell: Mrs., 45; Wallace, Dr., 45

Cosh: Delia, Miss, 2

Cossaboom, 93

Cottrell: Gershom, 102; Martha, Miss, 42; William H., 40

Courtney: Stephen, 3; Wm., 3

Covert: Elizabeth Ann, Miss, 9; John, 9; John H., 56

Coward: Anna E., 83; Anna M., Miss, 18; Charles A., 25, 27; George D., 19; George E., 82; George W., 1, 52; Miller, 39; Thomas, 82, 83

Cox: Adelaide, 41; Ann F., Miss, 8; George, 41; George H., 8; John M., 9; Kate, Miss, 83; Malvina A., Miss, 66; Richard, 36; Sarah, 11; Sarah, Miss, 87; William C., 65; Wm. H., 36

Craig: Carrie H., 78; D.N., 78; David N., 78; Kate R., Miss, 78; William H., 37

Crainhart: Sarah, 89

Crammer: Clayton, 101; Lizzie M., Miss, 79, 96; Wm., Esq., 79, 96

Crandall: T. Vaughn, 39

Cranmer: Isabella, Miss, 41; Wm. H., 83

Crawford: Aaron, 57

Crosby: Howard, Rev., 43

Croshaw: Charles A., 75; Samuel, 75

Crum: Rev., 79

Cubberley: Enos, 20; George Ely, 58; Voorhees, 22; Wesley, 20

Cubberly: Enoch, 42

Cueuel: Peter J., 18

Cummings: John, 82

Curley: Patrick, 62

Curry: Abnram, 91; Nathan S., 91

Cutter: Joseph, 72

(112)

INDEX

D

Daily: Anna, Miss, 79
Danley: Mr., 59
Danser: Charles, 79; Etta M., Miss, 79; Mary E., 98; Peter H., 98; Phoebe A., 101; Wesley, dec'd, 101
Davis, 70: Anna, 91; Charlotte, 101; George Henry, 7; J.B., Rev., 74, 78, 82, 86, 94, 97, 100, 104; John, 67; Mary E., Miss, 67; Robert, 91; Saxton, dec'd, 91; Sexton, dec'd, 91
Davison: Alice G., 22; Annie Amanda, Miss, 96; Catherine M., Miss, 87; Charles E., 22; Cornelia, Miss, 20; Daniel, 64; Edward R., 42; Ella, Miss, 95; Ellen, Miss, 46, 96; Ezekiel, 14; Franklin B., 88; Geo. W., 97; George, 20; Georgianna, Miss, 92; James C., , 95; Jane Ann, 104; John D., 37, 92; John S., 104; Lydia R., Miss, 76; M. Augusta, Miss, 7; Maggie A., Miss, 39; Margaret Ann, 22; Mary, 104; Mary, Miss, 55; Rebecca, 14; Ruth, 64; S.O., 38; Sylvanus, 46; Wm. D., 7; Wm. V.P., 37
Dawes: Aaron, 83, 84; Bertie, 83; Josephine, 83, 84; Nettie, 84
Dawney: William, 28
Daymond: Robert A. G., Esq., 12
Dayton: Dr., 88
Deacon: Henry W., 94
Deal: John F., 48
Dean: Mary J., 94
Debow: Elizabeth, 13; Margaret, 80; William, 24
Decamp: Elizabeth, Miss, 24
Decker, 74
Deitz: Charles M., Rev., 7

Denise: Daniel D., 89
Denison: Fannie C., Miss, 65; George, 65
Dennis: George, 26; Kathyrn, Ms., Intro; Wm. H., 63
Dey: Abby, 100; Abijah, 80; Acsah E., Miss, 55; Adelia, Miss, 96; Bertha, 80; David, 45; David B., Esq., 97; Derrick G., 7; Elmer P., 57; Euphemia M., 57; Ezekiel, 9; George S., 7; Hannah, Miss, 99; Isaac Scudder, 32; John M., 86; John S., 86; John W., 62; Jos. I., 61; Josie S., Miss, 21; Julia O., 94; Margaret E., 101; Margaret, Miss, 52; Martha A., Miss, 67; Matthew R., 55; Ralph A., 72; Ralph S., 67; Richard, 83; Ruliff S., 57; Sadie A., Miss, 97; Sarah Ann, Miss, 83; Seth, 52; Spafford W., 7; Taylor, 81; Thomas, 57; Voorhees, Lt., 26, 27; Wm. S., 21
Dickey: John, 78
Dillon: Ann, 91; Ezekiel, 91
Dippolt: Charles M., Jr., 46
Disborough: John, 8; Mary H., 8
Disbrow: Anna S., Miss, 49; Capt., 37; Emma, Miss, 67; H.S., Capt., 35, 49; Hendrickson, 67; Henry, 47; John L., 87
Ditmars: John, Capt., 14
Dobbins: Isaac, 85; J.R., 50
Dod: Albert B., Prof., 62
Dodd: Capt., 12; Rev., 12
Dolan: Mary, 4; Patrick, 4
Doley: James, 3
Donnel: James, 14; Mary, 14
Donnell: Mary E., 36
Donohue: Mrs., 86
Doolittle: Rev., 78
Doran: John, 98
Doremus: J.P., Mr., 87
Dow, 86

(113)

INDEX

Downs: Clarkson, 93; Elizabeth, 54
Dudley: Evan, Dr., 99
Duff: Thomas, 89, 97
Dugan: Thomas, 34
Duncan: George M., 95; John, 79; John S., 34; John W., 71; Kate, Miss, 79; Stephen, 34, 51; Ulsema, 34; Uselma, 2; Widow, 2; William, 7
Dunham: Curtis, 35, 36; Leonard W., 35, 36
Dunn, 72: Hugh, 22; Isaac, 68
Dye: Catharine, Mrs., widow, 58; Elias, 19; Harriet, Miss, 6; Lewis D., dec'd, 58; Sarah D., Miss, 5; Wm. P., 6

E

Eaches: O.P., Rev., 95, 97, 103, 104
Earl: Edward J., 54
Early: R. Morrison, 74
Eberhart: James, 75
Eckerson: Mr., 69
Eckley: Catharine, 65
Edsall: Ables, 80; Henry F., 100
Edwards: Caroline A., 12; Mary, Mrs., 97; Samuel, 97
Ege: S. Smith, 88; Sarah, 106; Smith, 106
Elbertson: Miller, 80
Eldridge: Aaron, 65; Obadiah, 65
Eldsley, 80
Elliot: Wesley T., 44
Ely: Abby A., Miss, 40; Adelaide, Miss, 55; Elizabeth L., 44; Elizabeth L., Mrs., widow, 40; Ellen, Miss, 6; George J., 105; John, 41; John H., 107; Jos. J., Esq., 97; Joseph S., 41; Lavinia, 11; Louisa C., Miss, 40; Patricia Davison, Intro; Richard, 40, 99; Richard R., 84; Sarah Matilda, Miss, 97; Thomas, 1; Thomas, Esq., 11; Thos., 40
Embley: Caroline, Miss, 8; David, 70; Elizabeth, 44; George, 44, 70, 72; Jesse, 9; Joseph, Esq., 8; Martin, 4; Rebecca, 70; William, 72
Emley: A.C., 24; A.J., 23; Andrew J., 23; Mary V., 24
Emmons: George, 44; James, 82; John, 49; Mary L., Miss, 82; Rebecca Ann, Miss, 39
English: Mary, 13; Nellie W., Miss, 58
Errickson: Angeline, Miss, 38; John J., 105
Ervin: Anna V., Miss, 104; George, 104; Joseph W., 67
Erwin: Elizabeth, 86; Joseph, 86; Sallie, 86
Evans: David, 1
Everett: B.S., Rev., 94, 95, 107
Everingham: James H., 43; Lydia Ann, 43
Evernham: James M., 11, 26, 27
Evert: Caroline, 91; George A., 91; Thomas, 91
Ewan: J., 97; Rebecca G., Miss, 97
Ewart: John, 100; Lydia, 59; Thomas, 59

F

Fairbank: J.N., Dr., 73, 105; Jennie E., Miss, 73
Fairchild: E.S., Rev., 105
Farr: Charles S., 43; Frederick, 68; George, 102; James, 67; Vincent C., 21
Farrell: James, Capt., 60
Faucett: William Francis, 47
Fellner: Sigismund, 4
Field: Ann M., Miss, 68; George R., 70; Richard Stockton, 86
Fielder: Geo. W., 98
Finlay: John, 94
Finney: S.L., Rev., 44
Fisher: Abijah C., 41; August, 49; George, 12; Helen, 12; James S., 96

(114)

INDEX

****

Fisk: David V., 67
Fitz Randolph: Thomas, Esq., 56
Fleming: Hartshorne, 66; Hartson, 63
Flock: Eliza, 55; J. Tindall, 55; Samuel, 45
Ford: Chas. M., 25; Mary, Miss, 74
Forman: Annie P., Miss, 65; James W., 69; John, Esq., 94; Nelson L., dec'd, 19, 43; R.R., 69; R.R., Esq., 65; Rachel A., Miss, 43; Sarah E., Miss, 19; Sarah, Miss, 83; Selah G., 21
Fort: Franklin G., 96
Foster: Ned, 53
Fountain: O.H., 58
Fowler: Mr., 50
Francis: Isaac, 60; Margaret, 70
Franklin: Robert, 69
Fraser: D.R., Rev., 17; John F., 60
Frelinghuysen: Theodore, Hon., 10

G

Gage: George, 64
Gamble: Sallie, Mrs., 78
Garnet: Mrs., 62
Garrison: C.F., Rev., 105; Garret, 63
Gaskill: Job, 71
Geary: Patrick, 82
Genreux: Mrs., 84
Giberson: Orpha, 65
Gifford: Emma J., 101
Gilbert: Wm., 4
Gill, 103
Gilliland: Wm., 104
Gilma: James A., 79
Gilmore: A., Rev., 24, 25
Glenbudd: Henry, 98
Glew: Edward Lees, 91
Goldy: Emeline, 28; Isaac H., 68; Isaac, Sr., 28; Kate, 68
Gordon: Benjam, 24; Benjamin, 78; David, 67; David, Sr., 51; Eliza Ann, Miss, 43; Furman, 53; Henry L., 18; Mercy A. H., 22; Sallie E., Miss, 24; Thomas F., Intro
Gorman: James, 25, 27
Grant: G. W., 11; Mary Anna, 11; Matilda, 11
Gravatt: Achsah C., Miss, 67; Henry C., 45; Jane, Miss, 66; Mary Ann, Miss, 53; Sarah E., 3; Thomas E., 107
Graw: J.B., Rev., 52
Greely: Thomas, 4
Green: Jesse, 13; Rachel Ann, Miss, 2
Greenbank: W.E., Rev., 79
Greenleaf: Joseph, Rev., 94; Margaret, 76; W.E., Rev., 96
Gregory: A.J., Rev., 107; George, 88
Gribens: John, 25, 27
Grier: Robert C., 90
Griffin, 89: George H., 58; Walter, 97
Griggs: Clarissa, Mrs., 46; Derrick, 20; George, 64; Henry M., 21; Joachim, 31; John S., 71; Margaret, 71; Orsemus, 64; Reuben, 63; Sidney, 20; Van Wickle, 31
Grove: Eliza J., Miss, 72; Emily H., Miss, 53; Samuel L., 53; Samuel S., 72; William, 53
Grover: Barzillai, 20; Cornelius, 72; David D., 6; Eleanor K., Miss, 6; H.C., 20; Hiram A., 38; John H., 103; Laura, Miss, 87; Mary, Miss, 20, 53; Susan. Mrs., 93; Sylvanus, 6, 53; Sylvanus, Jr., 83
Groves: C. Calvin, 97; Charles, 42; Charlott J., Miss, 80; Gideon, 80; John R., 86; Louisa A., Miss, 42
Gulick: Abraham, 93; Abram, 19; Groves, Mrs., 99; Kate, Miss, 97; Redford, 79; S., Dr., 97

INDEX

H

Haborn: Annie, 8; Robert, 8
Hackett: Patrick, 61
Haley: Lydia G., Miss, 39; Martha A., 19
Hall: Caldwell K., Gen., 86; Ellie N., Miss, 70; Elsworth, 40; George A., 59; J., Rev., 86; James B., 70; James D., 70; Thomas, 40; Watson, 53
Halloran: Mrs., 84; Thomas, 84
Halpin: John, 60
Halsted: Louisa, Mrs., 105; Wm., 105
Hamilton: Andrew, 50; Edward G., 82
Hance: Sarah, Mrs., 107; Wm., Rev., 107
Hand: John S., 19
Handley: Mary, 43
Hanes: Henry, 101
Hankins: Abigail, 93; Helena, 93; Zachariah, 93
Hankinson: Asher, 47, 48; David, 99; Lewis, 80
Harden: John, 73; Rachel, 73; William H., 41
Harker: Franklin M., 7
Harkness: James, 101
Harle: Henry E., 9
Harris: Alfred, Rev., 2; Susan, 71
Hart: A.C., 95; Enoch W., 106; Sarah Ann, Miss, 100
Hartman: Garrett, 73; Gilbert, 11; Hannah Margaret, 73; Sarah B., Mrs., 23
Hartranft: C.D., Rev., 40
Hartwell: P, Elder, 94; P., Elder, 88
Hassler: J.W., Rev., 61
Havins: Louisa, Miss, 106
Hawk: Daniel, 58; Mary Louisa, Miss, 58
Hay: Michael, 83
Hazleton: Benjamin, 83
Headley: J. Boyd, 89; Joseph, Capt., 89
Heiss: T. Taylor, Rev., 81, 106
Hendrickson: Charles D., 17; David, 4; Hannah, 4; John L., 67; Sarah Louisa, Miss, 67; Thomas, 15
Herbert: Sam F., 27; Samuel F., 26; Stephen, 85
Herron: Thomas J., 37; Wm. Reed, 37
Hewlett: S.M., Esq., 24
Hewson: Thomas, colored, 69
Hibbets: Ella, Miss, 96
Hibbetts: Maria M., Miss, 8; Peter D., 8
Hicks: John, 53; Samuel, 13
Hill: David, 4; Edwin, 55; Emily B., 4; James M., 83; Samuel S., 4, 10; Sarah A., 4; Theodore, 89
Hilliard: S.W., Rev., 22
Hillyer: Wm., 11
Hilton: Frances J., 22
Hires: W.D., Rev., 68; Wm. D., Rev., 52
Hoagland: Charles Edgar, 100; Derrick, 100; Sarah F., 100
Hoffman: Charlotte, Miss, 7
Holcombe: Anna Munro, 15; Ella W., 15, 57; Mr., 11; Samuel, 15, 56
Holeman: Anna, 103; James P., 10; Mary J., Miss, 63; Rebecca, 103
Holman: James, 25, 27; John H., 55; Kenneth, 99; Lewis I., 95; William H., 55
Holmdel: Jonathan, 33
Holmes: D.A., Mr., 83; Elizabeth, 75; Isaac H., 56; John, 13, 51; John R., 75; Obadiah, 33; William, 51
Hooper: Alfred F., 21; Mary B., Miss, 96; Thomas, 98; Thos., 22; William, 96
Hoover, 59: T.D., Rev., 18; Thomas D., Rev., 2, 22; Thos. D., Rev., 5, 6, 7, 8, 9, 19, 21, 37, 38, 39, 40, 42, 45, 46, 48
Hopkinson: Annie, 64; Francis, 64
Hopper: Carrie, Miss, 89
House: William E.H., 77
Howell: Arthur, 70; Tobias, 49; Wm. C., Esq., 72
Howland: Peter W., 90

(116)

INDEX

Howlet: Rev., 66
Hoy: Robert T., 48
Hubb, 28
Huff: William, 98
Hugh, 53
Hughes: Albert T., 22; Angelina, Miss, 55; Ezekiel, 11; G., Rev., 64, 70, 76, 77; George, Rev., 69; Lambert R., 58; Lewis D., 33; Lydia A.P., Miss, 58; Rev., 74; Vincent, 104
Hulet: Ezekiel, 7; Rachel, Miss, 7
Hulick: John M., 95
Hulit: Jane, 54; Romaine, 81
Hulsart: John I., 40
Hulse: Aaron, 10; Jane, 76; John, 76; Theodosia, Miss, 66; William, 66
Hulseman: Daniel, 75
Hunsinger: Charles S., 42
Hunt: Charles F., 43; Chas. F., 44; Georgiana, Miss, 5; Jane E., Miss, 22; Jonathan, 33; Joseph, Jr., 87; Joseph, Sr., 44; Mary Anna, Mrs., 44; Thomas, 61; Wilson G., 61; Wm. T., 61
Hurley: Hattie, Miss, 40
Hutchi[n]son: Deborah, 38; Richard, 38
Hutchinson: A.F., Rev., 50; Alfred, 44; Carrie R., Miss, 6; Daniel P., 73; Elizabeth, 21; Enoch, 55; Isaac, 65; John B., Rev., 55, 58; Jonathan E., 87; Judson, 55; Martha, 63; Matilda, Mrs., 1; Phebe, Mrs., widow, 38; S.[ylvester], Rev., 73; Sylvester, Rev., 38; Voorhees K., 6; William, 22, 63
Hyatt: J. Henry, 65

I

Ihrie: Charles J., Col., 39
Imlay: John, 21
Ingraham: Wm. I., 23

Ireland: Margaret A., Miss, 103
Irvin: Charles, 83; Cornelius, Mrs., 85; Edward, 83
Irwin: John, 79
Ives: Cornelius, 23; John, 23; Milton, 23
Ivins: Ann, Mrs., 89; Emma, 24; George W., 22; John, 24

J

Jackson: D., Rev., 57; William F., 89
Jaggers: Harriet, Miss, 105
Jay: J., Rev., 77
Jelf: Sally, 84
Jemison: Geo. H., 27; George W., 25; Jennie, Miss, 44; Peter A., 26, 27; Wm. H., 26, 27
Jewell: Mary, 5, 93; Wm. D., 93
Jimeson: Edwin, 21; Elias, 107; Joseph H., Esq., 18; Mary F., Miss, 18; Peter A., 11
Jimison: Elizabeth, Miss, 56
Jobes: Anna B., 63; Hannah M., 63; Judge, 63; Willie M., Miss, 56
Jobs: Mrs., 10
John, [colored], 89
Johnes: Charles, 11; Daniel, 11, 96; Samuel, 41; Sarah, Mrs., widow, 41; Stephen, 56
Johns: J.H., Rev., 66
Johnson, 89: Alsena E., 1; Anthony, 59; David S., 76; Henry, 95; J.C., Mayor, 87; J.R.C., Esq., 88; James, 101; Jane, Miss, 70; John, 16; John C., 1; John H., 105; Lydia F., Miss, 95; Margaret, 1; Martin, 106; Nicholas, 95; Robert, 90; Sarah A., Miss, 95; T.F., 35; Thomas, 35; William H., 43; Wm. B., 444
Johnston: Charles, 28; Mary F., Miss, 22;

INDEX

Phebe, 28
Jolly: Charlotte M., Miss, 6; Joseph, 30; Leititia, Miss, 6; Robert, 30, 37; Thomas, 37
Jones: J.C., Rev., 69; James T., 51; John, 79; Mary, 84; Stephen, 56; Theodore, 51; W.P., 69
Justice: Augustus, 5

K

Karcher: J., Rev., 106
Karsey: Bridget, 88
Kay: Samuel, 100
Kearney: Phillip, Maj. Gen., 13
Kears: Eliza, Mrs., 105
Keeler: A. Lincoln, 75; Charles, 75; Isaac, 12; Wm H., 61
Kehoo: J.L., Rev., 47, 58, 71, 94, 96
Kelley: John W., 74
Kelly, 89: Patrick, 30
Kennedy: Margaret, 40
Ker: Joseph, 44; Sarah C., 44
Kerr: Joseph, 94
Ketcham: K.P., Rev., 39, 42
Ketchum: K.P., Rev., 19; Kneeland, Rev., 21, 23; Rev., 67
Keys: Samuel, 87
King: Israel, 50; Maggie, Miss, 87
Kinsey: Hannah, Miss, 22
Kirby: Anna M., 7; Robert F., 63; Samuel, 88
Kirkbride: Melvina, Miss, 49
Kirkpatrick: J., Rev., 24
Kirtley: William J., 51
Klemaun: William, 92
Kline: David, 43
Knowles: Anna L., Miss, 46; Jacob, 46
Kohler: Mathias, 88
Konover: John V.D., 58; Margaret A.,, 46; Mary Ann, 45; Ralph, Esq., 45; Richard B., 46; Richard G., 46
Kunzick: Adolf, 13
Kusacabe: Taro, of Japan, 84

L

Labaw: Francis D., 35; George F., 35
Laird: Esther Ann, 54; George, 54; George K., 64
Lake: Alice A., Miss, 106; Caroline, Miss, 105; Daniel, 85; Emma J., Miss, 105; Oliver, 105, 106
Lalor: Jerry, 18
Lamberson: Jacob B., 22; Theodore, 9
Lamler: Mary, Miss, 62
Lane: Dr. L., 24; Edward T., 12; Helen M., 90; James B., Esq., 14; John, 77; Lizzie M., Miss, 24
Lanning: Cornelia, Miss, 101; Elizabeth, Mrs., 84; Jane, Mrs., 107; Nathaniel, 101; William, 71
Larew: Levi, Rev., 65, 66
Lavens: Annie, Miss, 62
Lawrence: R.V., Rev., 78
Lawson: Wm., 3
Layton: John, 78
Lehming: Charles, 12; Charles C., 27; Charles H., 25
Leland: Joseph S., 60
Lenhart: J. L., Rev., 9
Lewis: Albert, 101; Alfred, 81, 93, 101; Amanda, 93; Charles, 70; Charlotte M., Mrs., 68; David, 57; Garret S., 71; John, 81, 92; John H., 87; John L., 104; Lewis, 14; Merriet, 104; Merritt M., 95; Thomas, 70, 92
Liming: Mary R., Miss, 7
Little: James, 29

INDEX

Lloyd: James, Esq., 27; Mary Augusta, Miss, 27
Lockerby: D.F., Rev., 88, 101
Long: Gertrude C., Miss, 19; Wm., 19
Longstreet: Annie E., 64
Lot: Harry, 103; William, 103
Lott: Chas. H., 95; Wm. F., 57
Lowrey: John, Rev., 2, 46
Lucas: Carrie H., 99; Edward, 78, 99; John M., 83; Stella, 99
Ludlam: Providence, Senator, 56
Lutes: Martha J., Miss, 54; Wm. C., 54
Lyne: William, 106

M

Macdonald: J., Rev., 55
Magee: Hattie E., Miss, 107; Jos. C., Esq., 94; Joseph C., 107; Mary E., Miss, 94
Mallery: D.G., Rev., 44
Malsbury: John M., 4
Malusbury: Alice, Miss, 26
Manning: Robert S., Rev., 54
Maple: Ella, 90; Garrett, 83; Henry, 13; Hezekiah, 28; John, 13, 83
Maps: Michael, 1
Margerum: W., Rev., 49, 60, 66
Marks: William, 90, 92
Martin: Abbot, 90; James H., 90; Maria, 90; Mr., 83
Mathews: A., Rev., 63
Matthews: Mary Jane, Miss, 43
Maxwell: James M., Rev., 17
Mc Gowan: Henry, 101; Patrick, 101
McBride: Peter, 76
McCabe: George, 74, 105
McCarthy: Timothy, 69
McChesney: Hugh, 27; Joseph M., 15, 33; Lida, Mrs., 104; Lizzie, Miss, 15; Robt. R., 104; Thomas, 33; William, 27
McClintock: John, Rev., 82
McCluskey: John, Rev., 17
McCoy: Charles C., 101; Mary H., Miss, 47
McCullough: Mathew, 27
McDonald: Alexander, 78; Catherine Elizabeth, Miss, 21; Patrick, 17
McDougall: J.W., Rev., 23
McDowell: Andrew, 46; Geo. T., dec'd, 8; George, 57; George T., dec'd, 23; John T., 33; Mary A., Miss, 23; Sadie H., Miss, 66; Susan C., Miss, 8; Thomas, 33
McDowell, Esq.: George, 72
McGeorge: Wallace, M.D., 74
McIntire: John, 1
McKean: Mayor, 7
McKenna: Henry A., 54; James, 55
McKennis: Henry, 73; Mary Alice, 73
McLean: D.V., Rev., 77
McManus: Frances J., Miss, 49; James, 50, 81; Sarah, Miss, 44
McMichael: Morton, 60; W. W., Rev., 5
McMorran: John, Esq., 26; William S., 26
McMurran: Alice, 12; John, 69; Joseph, 12, 69, 96; Joseph Winfield, 12
McTowe: Elizabeth, Miss, 68
McWilliams: Officer, 16
Meredith: R.R., Rev., 64
Merrick: Fanny, Miss, 66
Merrill: Ellen, Miss, 98; Henry, 98
Merryfield, 86
Mershon: James B., 42
Mesick: Rev., 78
Messlor: John R., 93; V., Rev., 93
Meyer: Francis L., 60
Meyers: Mary, Miss, 39
Middleton: Kate, Intro
Mikels: William S., Rev., 51
Miller, 53: Arthur, 100; E. Augustus, Miss, 49;

(119)

INDEX

Henry W., 100; Mary V., Miss, 88; Robert W., 49; Sarah R., Miss, 7; Symmes H., 96
Mills: Edward, 19; Sarah A. E., Miss, 1
Mock: Jacob, 73, 74
Mohn: Miss, 50
Moore: George R., 81; Gussie, 81; Henry A., 6; Joseph M., 11; Maggie H., Miss, 98; Mary, 6; Mary E., Miss, 9; Samuel, 59
Morrell: Anna J., 72
Morris: Geo. K., Rev., 105; James B., Capt., 52, 94; Jeremiah C., 98; Johnnie Davis, 98; Mary E., 98; Mary E., Mrs., 100; S., Rev., 100; Stephen, 98; Thomas E., 58
Morrison: S.W., Dr., 66; Wm. T., Rev., 82
Morse: Garrett, 35; William, 35
Morton: Ruth A., Miss, 105
Mosher: David, 102
Mott: Sarah B., Miss, 10
Mount: Abijah, 78; Adaline E., Miss, 97; Alice, 90; Archibald F., 71; Britton, 7; C. W., Intro; Catharine, 16; Charles P., 90; Cornelia, Miss, 43; Emma, 16; Enoch, 9, 71; Ezekiel, 95; James, 5; John, 102; John F., 67, 99; John G., 23; John R., 19; John S., 23; Katy, 71; Mahala, 5; Mary Ann Amelia, Miss, 45; Mary J., Miss, 19; Melvina, Miss, 95; Mercy, Mrs., 3; Morgan F., Intro; Rebecca, Miss, 78; Samuel, 65; T.S., Mr., 84; V.W., 43; Wm., 16
Murphy: Holmes W., 5; J. Frank, 68; James, 75; Joseph, Esq., 39; Phebe, Miss, 39; William S., Mrs., 40
Myers: John, 66; Josephine A., Miss, 66

N

Nealy: Sarah M., Miss, 81; Thomas, 81
Neary: Wm. H., 105
Neilds: W.F., Rev., 27
Newbold: Alex, 84
Newbury: Tyler E., 75; Zilpha E., Miss, 75
Newell: Ex-Gov., 76; William D., Dr., 76
Newman: Ann W., Miss, 92; Geo. H., 105
Newton: Almira, Miss, 71; Sallie, Miss, 105
Nicholson: Hattie B., Miss, 55
Nightengale: William, 75
Nixon, 80
Norcross: C.M., Mr., 60; W.W., 24
Norris: Emma, 3; Emma, Miss, 40; George, 106; J.C., Hon., 102; James C., 1, 10; Lawrence T., 96; Lilly Irene, 10; Matilda, 10; Mulford, 106; Reuben, 3
Norton: Annie, Miss, 21; C. M., Intro; Frances, 14; Helen, Miss, 69; Louise, 14; Wicoff, 14; William C., 60; Wyckoff, 94
Nutt: Lizzie, Miss, 104; Mr., 46; Sallie A., Miss, 57; Samuel, 104; William, 53

O

O'Neil: Daniel, 50
Oakerson: Anna, Miss, 66; David, 66
Ocermiller, 80
Odenheiner: Bishop, 48
Ogborn: Elizabeth N., 21; Hattie W., Miss, 74; Joseph, 52; Martin L., 70, 93; Mary, 93; R.J., 21; William, 52; William J., 93
Ogden: James, 58, 60; Rachel, Mrs., 60
Orr: Rev., 94

INDEX

P

Packer: Melville, 73; Theodore, 67; William H., 73

Page: Anna M., Mrs., 38; E. Cole, 38; Edward, Rev., 46; Joseph, 78

Palmer: Clayton, 1; Edward, 79; Mrs., 79

Pancoast: Emily, Miss, 85

Parent: Edward, 54

Parker: Charles, 60; Conductor, 77

Parmelee: D.S., Rev, 39; D.S., Rev., 17, 38; Mary Adelaide, Miss, 39

Patterson: James M., 70; James, Hon., 48; Joseph W., 7; Mariah, Miss, 5

Paxton: James, 86; John R., 6; Margaret, 80; Theodosia, Mrs., 39

Pearce: Israel, 8; Israel, Esqr., 100; Martha, 100; Mary, 8; Wm., 49

Peckham: Anna M., Miss, 24; Peckham, Rufus, Esq., 24

Peer: Ellen, 4

Pembrook: Ada, 51; Charles, 73; Chas. H., 51; Orian, 73

Peppler: John L., 21

Perkins: H., Rev., 5

Perrine, 17: Alfred, 11, 68; Alfred S., 31; Ann, Mrs., 87; Anna, 103; Augustus, Maj., 76; Barclay, 10; Beakman, 19; Charles H., 99; D.C., 17; Daniel W., 2, 3, 62; David, 34; David K., 92; David W., 51; Edward B., 63; Elijah, 22; Elijah V., Esq., 87; Forman, 29; George, 104; Harriet L., 71; Henry, 11, 19, 34; Isaac, 40; J. Barclay, 77; Jacob, 22; Jennie, Miss, 87; John, 100; John A., Gen., 76; John Albert, 51; John E., 1; John E., dec'd, 8; John H., 31; John, Maj., 8; Jonathan S., 7; Joseph, 70; Kate H., 80; Lewis, 12; Lizzie, 62; Lydia D., 94; Margaret, Miss, 53; Marianna, 40; Mary A., 61; Mary A., Miss, 7; Mary E., 2; Matilda Ann, Miss, 25; Matthew, 63; Matthias M., 7; Miss, 84; Peter, 41; Phebe, Miss, 68; Rebecca E., Miss, 19; Robert, 34; Samuel Ely, 8; Sarah, 8; Sarah I., Miss, 8; Spafford, 34; Stephen J., 95; Thomas E., 107; Thomas J., 39; Vincent, 5; William, 53; William D., 97; William H., 71; Wm., 61, 104; Wm. J., 65

Peters: Anna E., Miss, 102; Mary, Miss, 103

Peterson: B.H., Dr., Intro

Petherbridge: Ida Ruthetta, 39; J.B., Dr., 39; John B., Col., 46; John B., Dr., 39; Lizzie A., 39; R. Martin, 37

Pettie: Jacob C., 21

Pettit: Rev., 102

Petty: Nelson, 73; William H., 6

Pew: William, 41

Pharo: Joseph W., Hon., 10

Phelp: J.S., Rev., 98

Phelps: B., Rev., 53; J.S., Rev., 86, 93, 100, 104, 105, 106

Picton: Rev., 62

Pierce: Alice, Miss, 70; Henry, 14; Stephen, 73

Pierson: Catherine, Miss, 7; John S., 7

Pillow: George W., 85

Pippenger: Charles, 15; Daniel, 15; Ruliff H., 15

Pittenger: Adelia, 16; Daniel, 16

Pittman: Jacob, 46

Platt: Charles, 71

Post: S.E., Rev., 16, 18, 20, 67

Potts: Abigail, Mrs., 43; Thomas, 35; William A., 12

Powell: Henriette, Miss, 65

Pratt: J.C., Rev., 82

Prevo: Andrew M., 56

Price: A.E., Miss, 101; Jos. S., 11; William, 2

(121)

INDEX

Prickett: Edwin C., 79, 96
Priest: Annie E., 82; R.R., 82
Pritchard: Dr., 1; Kittie N., Miss, 69; M. Louise, Miss, 1
Proctor: John, 92
Provost: Cornelius, 29; David, 29
Pullen: Adaline, Miss, 20; Adelaide V., Miss, 46; Alexander, 69; Alfred, 10; Anna F., Miss, 74; Barzillai, 50; Carrie, Miss, 21; Chalis, 82; Charles, 37; Cordelia, Miss, 12; DeWayne, 69; Embley, 104; Emma H., Miss, 60; Enoch, Esq., 21, 46; Frank A., 55; Freeman R., 3; George E., 23; Isaac, 12, 54, 57; Isaac, Hon., 74; J. Madison, 56; Johnson, 88, 106; Lizzie, 82; Lydia Ann, 104; Mary, Miss, 38; Sallie E., Miss, 88; Samuel M., 98; Samuel T., 59; Sarah, 106; Sarah P., 59; T.J., 80; T.J., Esq., 90; Wm. HJ., 37
Purdy: Charles, 42; Israel Carl, 61; Joseph H., 102; Robert, 61, 102

R

Rahl: Hessian Commander, 10
Rake: Ramsey, 96
Ralph: Sarah, Miss, 66
Randolph: Ann, Mrs., 83; L.B., Mr., 99; Mary, Miss, 83
Rankin: James, Capt., 64
Raymond: George, 28
Read: Edgar W., 56
Reamer: James, 11, 25, 27
Reddick: John, 48; John A., 49; John, colored, 41
Redfield: Ellery C., 15
Redman: Jesse, 40
Redmond: Robert, 52
Reed: Abraham, 89; Azariah, 42, 53; Charles, 89; Eleanor F., 96; Elizabeth, Miss, 1; Eveline, 106; Grandon, 106; Hannah, Miss, 42; James C., 46; Jonathan F., 17; Joseph, 3; Lawrence, 65; Sarah, Mrs., 52; Wm. B., 35
Reed (colored), 73
Reeve: P. Fidelia, 95; W.B., Rev., 95
Reid: Charlotte M., 68; John, 43; Wm. I., 68
Relyea: Clifford Baldwin, 13; M., Rev., 4, 9, 13; Milton, Rev., 1
Reynolds: Julia, Mrs., 94
Rhoades: James, 32; John, 32; L.J., Rev., 24
Rice: Anna, colored, 68
Richardson: Benjamin, 99; Emma, 76; James B., 16; Schuyler, 76; William B., 16
Riggs: D.B., 62; Elias, Esq., 42, 59; Lewis L., 62; Marsena, Mr., 104; Reuben, 1
Righter: Stephen, Mr. & Mrs., 84
Rivers: Joseph, colored, 41
Robbins: Aaron, 1; Annie, Miss, 7; Charles, 74; Charles L., 18, 51; D.W., Mr., 87; F., Rev., 13; Henry W., 58; Isabella, Mrs., 22; Jane L., 18; John F., 55; Jonathan, 2; Mary, Miss, 74; R.C., 38; Randal C., 15; Sgt., 11
Robert: Austin W., 31
Roberts: Daniel, 17; Emma F., 104; Manuel, 92; Thomas, Rev., 17
Robinson: Abram, 105; John A., 39; John T., Esq., 39; Martin V., 26, 27
Rock: Edmund [colored], 88
Rodgers: Cornelia W., Miss, 66
Rogers: Charles A., 49; Charles S., 107; Dr., 89; Edith W., Miss, 44; Geo. L., 76; Hattie A., 77; Henry A., 39; Jefferson H., 30; Lydia, 102; Margaret N., Miss, 21; Mary H., Mrs., 17; Meloine, Miss, 44; Oscar F., Esq., 44; Samuel M., 95; Vanroom, 77; W.D., 26, 27
Roman: Henry C., 18
Romand: Mr., 70

INDEX

Rose: Henry, 74
Rosler: William, 92
Rossell: Amanda, 6; Isaac, 6, 21; Jane, Miss, 21; N. B., Maj., 12
Roszell: Charles, 47, 52; Charles R., 53; Hannah, 47
Roth: Charles, 45; Joseph, 36
Rowe: J. Temple, Rev., 106
Rowland: Isaac B., 42; J., 14
Ruding: Arthur, 100; Martha, 100; Mary Virginia, Miss, 7; Virginia, Mrs., 16; Wm., 7
Rue: Austin, 87; Cornelius, 10; Daniel Johnes, 16; Edmond, Esq., 107; Ellen, 96; Enoch, 15, 67; Enoch Allen, 68; George, 17; Harvey P., 16; J.E., Rev., 41, 89; Jennie A., Miss, 100; John Henry, 32; Joseph E., 42; Lizzie M., 17; Mary E., Miss, 107; Rebecca, 103; Rebecca E., Miss, 15; Samuel, 16; William, 103; William E., 94; William S., 42; William, Jr., 79; Wm. Price, 32
Runyon: Peter F., 106
Rusher: C.H., Mr., 105; Elizabeth Jane, Miss, 105
Russell: Clara, Miss, 69

S

Sailer: John, 71
Saley: Anna Adelia, Mrs., 20; John, 18; Melville, 18, 20; Melvin, 46
Sands: Mary Louisa, Miss, 38
Sanford: Henry, 47; John W., 18
Savage: George, 57
Savidge: J.D., 20
Savige: Edward, 60; Theodosia, Mrs., 68
Sayre: Wm. R., 93
Scattergood: John H., 5

Scelover: Abraham I., 23; Emily A., Miss, 23; Wm. Reed, 8
Scheibe: Oskar, 97
Schenck: Ezekiel, 43; John H., 95; Maria D., Miss, 5; S. Mount, Esq., 27
Schetky: G.P., Rev., 56
Schultz: John, 41
Schuyler: Daniel, 44; Ellen, Miss, 54; Mary Ann, Miss, 43; Mary Anna, 44
Schwand: Leonard, 81
Schwartz: Mrs., 79
Schwenger: Mary Ann, Mrs., 45
Scott: James, 15; Mary, Miss, 64
Scranton: James P., 39
Scudder: Ella M., Miss, 27; James, 27
Seaman: Gilbert, Capt., 74
Sears: Rev., 91
Seger: J., Rev., 56; John, Rev., 93
Selover: W.R., 20
Serull: James (Negro), 75
Serviss: David N., 31; Georgietita, 31; Naria L., Miss, 69
Shangle: Elizabeth, Mrs., 67; S., Esq., 93
Sharp: B.S., Rev., 58; James Robinson, 107; Sarah Elizabeth, 107; Sarah Jane, 107; Wm. Rev., 107; Wm., Rev., 107
Sherman: James T., 11; Mary, Mrs., 94
Shields: Patrick, 26, 27
Shinn: Vashti B., Miss, 82
Shippen: Richard, 60
Shotwell: Thomas, 81
Shreiver: S.S., Rev., 64
Shreve: Ralph H., 63
Shriver: S.S., Rev., 17, 39, 45, 46, 70
Sickles, 88: Sydney, 56
Silver: Wm. D., 97
Silvers, 4: Amanda, Miss, 8; Benjamin, 34; C.N., 14; Charles H., 25; Clark H., 30, 100; Clark H., Esq., 8; Elizabeth S., 6; Elwood, 29, 80; Elwood R., 26, 27;

INDEX

****

Gilbert, 29; Henry, 27; James N., 72; John, 78, 80; John H., 69; John S., 65; Nelson, 72; Nelson, Esq., 14; William H., 34
Simminds: John, 6
Simmons, 53
Sinclair: Joseph C., 55
Sisco: David, 80
Skillman: Jacob, 19
Skimins: Lizzie S., Miss, 92
Slater: F.A., Rev., 40
Slocum: David, 76
Slover: William R., 38
Smallset: John S., 66
Smith: I., Rev., 7, 8; Isabella, Miss, 102; James, 2, 86; Job, 3; Joseph, 69; L., Rev., 1, 2, 6, 9, 11; Lavinia, Miss, 47; Margaret M., Miss, 1; R. M., Col., 12; Sidney, 98; Sophie M., 98; Thomas, 31; William Johnes, 12; William, colored, 68
Smock: William, 93
Snedeker: Aaron, 81; Alex. C., 8; Catharine V., Miss, 8; David, 37; Emmaline, Miss, 23; Firman, 21; Geo. E., 97; Henry, 49; Isaac G., 9; Isaac J., 68; Jacob, 21; James B., 29; Laura, Miss, 68; Peter, 29; Sarah B., Miss, 18; T. Salter, Esq., 18, 62; Thomas Sorter, 34
Snyder: J.L., 9
Soden: Garret N., 69; Jane, Miss, 106; Lydia J., Miss, 43
Sodon: William H., 31
Solomon: Levi, 6
Somers: Dermond, 9
Sone: Jacob, 68
Sonnard: Cook S., 61
Soutell: Charles, 88
Sovereign: Frederick W., 14; Thomas, Rev., 14
Sparks: Anna, Miss, 58; Thomas, Esq., 58
Spear: Augustus, 55; Sarah E., 55

Sprague: Joel M., 41
Spurling: Caroline, Miss, 37
Stackhouse: Chas., 40
Stahl: Conrad, 81
Stanger: G.C., 96
Stanleup: Wm. M., Rev., 102, 103
Steele: Charles W., 47; John M., 68
Stelle: George, 4
Stephenson: Alfred, 55; Mabel, 55; Wm. L., 78
Stevens: Edward A., 62; John, Col., 62; Thos., Rev., 69
Stevenson: Alfred, 16, 70, 72, 74; Anna J., 72; Emma J., Miss, 70; James W., 16
Steward: Mary Elizabeth, 60; Charles, 47
Stewart: Allen, 42; Clara, Miss, 42; Robert, 2; Rosalie A., Miss, 77
Stile: George, 24
Stiles: Mary E., 90
Stillwell: Daniel P., 19; Elmira, Miss, 14; J.B., 14
Stockson: Sarah, 42
Stockton: Charles, 42; Harriet M., 10; J.H., Rev., 77, 78; R. F., Com., 10; Richard, 38; Robert Field, Commodore, 38
Stonaker: Alfred, 43; Clarence S., 73; David, 9; John, 73; Lydia J., Miss, 43; Rebecca, Miss, 9
Stoneberger: A.S., Dr., 79
Stout: Amelia W., Miss, 80; Annie, Mrs., 64; Charles, 80, 81; Charles R., 31; Joseph, 31; Lizzie J., Miss, 81; William J., 55
Street: A.K., Rev., 17, 19; Frank A., 17; Sallie Irene, Miss, 19
String: Wm., 19
Strong: Adele, Miss, 57; C., Mr., 57; Richard, 90
Stryker: John J., 22
Studdiford: Samuel M., Rev., 101
Stults: Andrew J., 51; Arthur V., 9; Catharine A., Miss, 43; Catharine, Mrs., 53;

INDEX

****

Cornelius B., 8; E., Miss, 23; E.D., Rev., 92, 100, 106; Harriet, Miss, 102; Henry A., 19; Isaac, 23, 43; Isaac S., 30; J., Mr., 76; Jacob, Intro; Jacob H., 51; John, 53; John Edgar, 97; Marcus Aurelius, 30; Mary A., Miss, 67; Peter, 34; Peter P., 66; Sarah Elizabeth, Miss, 97; Sarah Jane, 66; Sarah S., Miss, 19; Simeon M., 19; Sorter S., 34; Susan A., Miss, 53; Symmes H., Capt., 30; Symmes Henry, 30; T. Saulter, 97; Thomas S., 67; Thomas Sorter, 30; William, Jr., 46; Wm. N., 2

Stultz: E.D., Rev., 72; L.D., Rev., 87
Sutton: Nathan C., 82
Sweeney, 75
Swett: W.W., Mr., 102
Swift: Lavina C., 5; Thomas C>, 74
Sykes: Clarence W., 38
Symmes: J.G., Rev., 23, 27, 43, 95, 97; J.S., Rev., 8; Jos. G., Rev., 7, 19, 23, 49, 56, 80, 97; Jos.G., Rev., 22, 81; Joseph G., 101; Joseph G., Rev., 52, 55, 67, 68, 71, 78, 79, 105
Symonds: George W., 70

T

Taggart: Daniel, Intro
Tantum: Amos, 15; Elizabeth, 58; J.A., 23; Maria, 15; Rebecca, Miss, 45
Taylor: Ann M., Miss, 94; Augustus M., 91; Charles J., 66; Clayton, 4; Cornelia, Miss, 42; Edward C., Intro; Elenor, 71; George W., Gen., 13; George, Dr., 50; Israel B., dec'd, 40; James, 42; John I., 71; John, Esq., 94; Joseph M., 87; Mr., 92; R., Rev., 2; R., Rev., 1, 5; T. R., Rev., 5

Teale: Charles E., 104
Tennent: William, Rev., 28
Terhune: Andrew, 43
Terry: Elizabeth, 47; Mary A., Miss, 38
Thomas: Abel C., Rev., 12; Alicia, Miss, 68; Anna J., Miss, 78; Daniel, 90; E., Miss, 23; Gilbert, 68; John, 23; John J., 56; Lydia Ann, Miss, 56
Thomason: Henry P., 5
Thompson: Ann Augusta, Miss, 9; Geo., 27; Geo., Sgt., 25; Gertrude S., Miss, 98; James, 103; Job P., 80; John, 11, 36; John, Esq., 17; Joseph, 36; Maggie, Miss, 2; N.D., Captain, 85; Nancy, Miss, 105; Senator, 14; Stephen E., 107; Thomas, 20
Thorn: R., Rev., 43
Throckmorton: M.H., 90
Tibbs: Emma, 28; Thomas L., 75; Thos. L., 28
Tice: Elias, 102
Tieman: John, 98
Tilton: Elisha, Mr., 106; Emily, 60
Tindal[l]: Amos, Esq., 98
Tindall: Amos, Esq., 98; Amy, Miss, 98; Garret S., 52; John W., 44; Theodore, 97; Willie, 52
Tobins: Liscomb T., 76
Trent: O.F., 53
Trough: Henry, 62
Truax: John W., 102
Truex: Jane, Miss, 106
Tulley: Thomas, 8
Tunis: Edward, 2
Turbin: J.B., Rev., 65
Turpin: Rev., 70

U

Updike: Anna L., 91; Chas. G., 19; Ebenezer

INDEX

C., 66; Elias, 66; Joanna, Miss, 95; John W., 87; Joseph, 91; Maggie, Miss, 66; Sarah, 95; William, 91
Updyke: Eli, 3; Levi C., 56

V

V-------: Miss, 31
Van Doren: Henry, 30; John Henry, 30
Van Duesen: Catharine J., Miss, 87
Van Dusen: Elwood, 59
Van Dyke: J.S., 97; J.S., Rev., 83, 96
Van Hise: Thomas, 31
Van Horn: H., 21; Sarah, Miss, 21; Thomas, 50; William, 96
Van Houten: Noah, 92
Van Kirk: Caroline, 71; John S., 71; Lawrence, 71
Van Marter: Cornelia, 103; David, 103; Elizabeth, widow, 58; Krion, 58
Van Name: Abby, 64; John, 64, 67
Van Nortwick: F., 81
Van Nosten: Augustus, 2
Van Pelt: Jacob, 68; John, 53
Van Sickel: Chester, 19
Van Syckel: P.B., Rev., 15
Vanarsdale: Jacob, 52
Vancleaf: Melissa, Miss, 17
Vanderveer: Aaron S., 40; D. Augustus, 5; G., 20; J. Calvin, 5; John C., 45
Vandewater: A.V., Rev., 44; Peter, 45
Vandusen: John E., 92
Vanhorn: Mary J., Miss, 20
Vankirk: Mr., 62
Vanleer: W.B., 57; W.B., Rev., 98, 105
Vannest: Abraham, 97; Emma, Miss, 107; J. Bergen, Mr., 107; John B., 96; Lydia C., Miss, 96
Vaughan: Kate A., Miss, 9

Vaughn: Henry, 8; Israel, 101; James G., 58, 90; Lewis, 64; Mary J., 64; Sarah, Miss, 57
Veghte: Theodore, 45
Vescelieus: William Austin, 101
Vibbert: G.H., Rev., 74
Vleit: Cornelius, 105
Von Emburg: Abraham, 49
Voorhees: Abram, dec'd, 81; Ada, Miss, 81; Alfred H., 35, 37; Charles, 56; Cornelia A., 56; Court, 22; George, 67; Hannah, Miss, 41; Joseph, 91; Joseph, Rev., 36, 78; Martin, Esq., 75; Peter, 56; R. Coates, 27; Rebecca, Miss, 78; Robert Coates, 35, 36; Stepehen, 95
Vreeland: Cornelius, 35; Mary M., Miss, 39; William, 35
Vroom: George A., 6

W

Waddy: Rebecca, 52; Richard, 52
Wainwright: Henry, 100; Joseph, 90; Mary E., 70
Wakeley: William A., 60
Wakely: William Andrews, 86
Walker: Jacob, Mrs., 99; James, 43; O. T., Rev., 10; W. Wilburforce, 95
Wall: James T., Hon., 48; Mary R., Miss, 48
Walling, 6
Waln: Nicholas, 94
Walters: Henry, 54; Josephine B., Miss, 51
Walton: Adaline, 51; Catharine, 92; Elizabeth, Miss, 77; Frank, 51; Rosteen, 51; William, 3, 51, 92
Ward: William V., Hon., 28
Ware: John, 99
Warren: Mrs., 89
Warwick: Annie, 46; William, 46

INDEX

Waterman: George, 61
Waters: E., Rev., 42; George, 1; James, Rev., 69; Philemon, 94
Watkinson: W.E., Rev., 45, 55, 57
Watson: H., Rev., 99, 101, 105; Rev., 59
Way: E.J., Rev., 48; Joseph L., 48
Webster: Joseph B., 2
Wells: W.M., 22; W.M., Rev., 43; William M., Rev., 98
Wescott: H., Rev., 40, 78
West: Anna P., Miss, 104
Westcott: J. Frank, 78
Westervelt: Eliza F., Mrs., 67
Wetherill: Forman P., 97
Whipple: Thomas D., Esq., 64
White: Isaac, 59; Isbella, Miss, 81; Jonathan D., 80
Whitemore: Ella K., Miss, 106
Whitlock: James, 72; Mary Ellen, 72; Mr., 100
Whitmore: Hannah Margaret, 73; John K., Esq., 73
Whittick: Charles, 98
Wickoff: Andrew Jackson, 81
Wicoff: John I., 46
Wideman: John, 62
Wilbur: Anna W., Miss, 95; Caroline, 9; Edward, dec'd, 95; James, 9; L., Dr., 9; Wm. A., Rev., 49
Wiley: Gerardus W., 100; Symmes H., 8
Wilgus: Mary, 67
Williams: Jane A., Miss, 16; John, 25, 27; Joseph, 48; Joseph, colored, 49; Lena A., Miss, 23; Mary, Mrs., 21; Sarah, Miss, 57; Sidney W., 7; Sittira Amanda, Miss, 54
Williamson: Elbert S., 31; Lemuel, 3; Mary E., 56
Willmarth: I.H., Rev., 97
Wills: Addie, Miss, 42
Wilson: Ann, Mrs., 103; Benj. O., 24; Charles, 16; Elizabeth, 104; Ezekiel, M.D., 107; Frank, 25, 27; Gertrude, 57; Hannah V., 42; Isaac H., 23; John, 103; Kate R., 77; Lydia Helen, Miss, 107; Morgan, 18; Peter, 57; Peter E., 6, 28; Rachel, 28; Rachel A., 6; William, 27; Wm., Capt., 52
Winant: Ann, 65; Gilbert, 92; Sidney, 65
Winchester: Asa F., 33; Perly F., 33
Winet: Mary Eliza, Miss, 60
Winner: I., Rev., 6; Isabella H., Miss, 50; Rev., 61
Wolf: John, 2
Wood: George W., 66; James, Rev., D.D., 47
Woodhull: A.W., Dr., 77; G.T., Judge, 77; John T., Dr., 77; John W., Dr., 43
Woolley: William, 63; William N., 66
Worrell: C.F., Rev., 14, 53, 57, 66, 73, 75, 78, 95, 98; Henry M., Prof., 95
Wright: Hendrickson, 102; John G., 18
Wyatt: Huldah A., Mrs., 93
Wyckoff: Eliza V., Miss, 65; James, 65; James V., 96; Mrs., 99; Peter, 38; William, 38
Wycoff: D. Baird, 95; Lydia Ann, Miss, 95

Y

Yard: Benjamin F., 17; James, Intro
Yeates: James, 48; Sally, 48
Young: Gabriel, 91; James, 66

Z

Zelwick: Elizabeth N., 46
Zerwick: John, 67

www.ingramcontent.com/pod-product-compliance
Lightning Source LLC
Chambersburg PA
CBHW080453170426
43196CB00016B/2785